To Steve

THE
POWER
TO FORGIVE

With blessings

1-2012

THE
POWER
TO FORGIVE

How to Overcome
Unforgiveness
and Bitterness

REINHARD HIRTLER

DESTINY IMAGE® PUBLISHERS, INC.

P.O. Box 310, Shippensburg, PA 17257-0310

"Speaking to the Purposes of God for this Generation and for the Generations to Come."

This book and all other Destiny Image, Revival Press, Mercy Place, Fresh Bread, Destiny Image Fiction, and Treasure House books are available at Christian bookstores and distributors worldwide.

For a U.S. bookstore nearest you, call 1-800-722-6774.

For more information on foreign distributors, call 717-532-3040.

Or reach us on the Internet: www.destinyimage.com.

ISBN 10: 0-7684-2821-1
ISBN 13: 978-0-7684-2821-6

For Worldwide Distribution, Printed in the U.S.A.

1 2 3 4 5 6 7 8 9 10 11 / 13 12 11 10 09

Dedication

I dedicate this book to all the hurting, wounded, and abused people who have suffered emotional pain, heartache, and agony. To those who are willing to push through their pain, break out of their prisons of unforgiveness and offence, and become the free people God has created them to be—you are the true heroes of the faith!

Acknowledgments

To my wife, Debi. Thank you for believing in me. Without your constant encouragement, this book would have never been written. Every time I felt like giving up, your words of encouragement pushed me forward. What a joy it is to continually take risks for the Kingdom of God together with you. What an amazing wife and friend the Lord gave me in you.

To my sons, Danny and Chris. You are great sons. Thank you, Danny, for reading the manuscript and for your valuable suggestions. Thank you, Chris, for your patience while I spent so many hours writing this book. I love you both!

To Nuffi. For your "stubborn encouragement" over many years concerning this project.

To John and Lisa. John, what a friend I found in you; you are so gentle and wise. Thank you for your helpful thoughts and insights. Lisa, thank you for your words of wisdom, not just concerning this book, but also into my life. Your depth and wisdom never cease to amaze me. In times of doubt, both of you believed in me and in this book.

To Tony and Nancy. You opened your home to us and showered us with love and grace. Thank you for letting me use the cabin to write this book. Tony, thank you for refreshing me by giving me your time when I need to relax.

To my best friend, Gerhard. God blessed me beyond words with your faithful friendship. You have a special place in my heart. Elfriede, thank you for lending me your husband so many times without complaining and being such a good friend to me and Debi. Christina, Hannah, and Samuel, thank you for always welcoming me and sharing your home with me.

To Ed and Enid. Ed, thank you for reading the manuscript. Thank you both for always loving us so unconditionally and for years of faithful friendship.

To Mike and Nicole. Mike, thank you for taking time out of your busy schedule and reading through the manuscript. Your encouragement meant so much to me—it came at a difficult time. Nicole, thank you for your refreshing smile and your sensitive heart.

To David and Amanda. Thank you for reading through these pages and giving me your feedback. Your passion for the Kingdom is inspiring and refreshing.

To Rob. Thank you for taking the time to read the manuscript and giving me your feedback. You have inspired me often. Words you spoke over two decades ago are still with me.

To Wolfi. Every time I met with you I left encouraged and inspired. You blessed me more than you realize. Thank you for reading the manuscript.

To Linda. You constantly pour your love into us. Words cannot express what you have done for us. Thank you for reading the manuscript.

To Mutti and Vati. You raised me in the ways of the Lord and faithfully prayed for me. You didn't give up when I almost ran away from the Lord in my pain. I love you dearly.

To Mom. You are my favorite mother-in-law. Even if you weren't my only one, you still would be my favorite one. I love you, Mom.

To Marco. Your willingness to help with this book blessed me.

To all my wonderful Christian friends in Austria—too many to name. You graciously opened your lives to me and allowed me to be part of your journey. You are some of the most amazing people in the world.

To my Lord Jesus. You never left me, never gave up on me, always taught me Your ways so lovingly. You healed my pain and gently, patiently led me on the road of life. I would not want to live one minute of my life without You. I love You with every fiber of my being.

Endorsements

A must-read for those wanting to come out stronger on the other side of betrayal, abuse, disappointment, and loss. Readers will be greatly encouraged by Reinhard Hirtler's practical insights and deep compassion. He takes us beyond the path of healing to the land of victory over every affliction of the soul.

John Hansen
Comptroller, MorningStar Ministries
Author, *The Vision That Changed a Nation*

One of the biggest battles facing the people of God today is that of unforgiveness and bitterness. Marriages, families, and churches are being divided, and countless people are being robbed of the fullness of God in their lives by this common enemy. *The Power to Forgive,* by my friend Reinhard Hirtler, contains some of the most helpful insights on this crucial subject that I have ever read. This book identifies open doors that have given unforgiveness and bitterness access into our lives, and it exposes the dangers of harboring these ruthless enemies. The wisdom found in these pages will help you navigate through the process of receiving the Father's healing and restoration in your own heart.

Mike Roberts, Assistant Pastor
MorningStar Fellowship Church
Wilkesboro, North Carolina

Through a wonderful blend of vivid illustration, story telling, penetrating questions, practical advice, personal testimony, and biblical wisdom, Reinhard Hirtler, in his new book *The Power to Forgive*, inspires us to take a healthier and deeper look at our lives and relationships to see if we are being weighed down by the tragedy of unresolved bitterness and resentment. I cannot think of a more profound and universal subject—forgiveness—to address, because it too often receives only superficial treatment by various cultures within today's society. It becomes immediately apparent that Reinhard won't allow us to settle for a surface solution as he appeals to us out of both his rich personal and pastoral experience. He helps us to desire to penetrate deeper regions of our hearts to ferret out any such enemies that may, openly or secretly, be gnawing away at our joy in Christ and what He has done for us in His incarnation, life, death, resurrection, ascension, and the outpouring of His Spirit upon us. May we all discover the grace of God to overcome the bitterness of this world that is such a terrible poison to our souls. Thank you, Reinhard, for serving us the sound and practical wisdom you have learned to help us gain greater and lasting freedom through Jesus Christ.

Michael Sullivant
Author, speaker, church leader

Contents

Foreword

I first met Reinhard in January 1992 in England at a pastors and leaders conference. There was an immediate connection in the Spirit, and even though we were on separate continents for more than a decade, we still kept in contact with each other. I was very excited when he told me he was moving to the United States.

If there is one sentence to describe Reinhard, it would be that his zeal for the Lord and the Kingdom of God is infectious. I think you will feel that in this book. He has a real passion for Jesus and for God's Kingdom to come here on earth.

In our own pursuit of passion for Jesus and doing our best to love Him as He deserves, we sometimes find hindrances in our lives that keep us from getting as close to Him as both He and we desire. There seems to be a lot of confusion in our lives and frustration as to why this is so. And indeed there is more than one answer to this ever-pervasive question in the Body of Christ.

Reinhard addresses one very good reason for our lack of nearness to Him, and sometimes even our own sense of loneliness.

Reinhard is not just teaching something out of the Bible, although there is nothing wrong with that. In my opinion, he is very qualified to do so. But in this book he is teaching something from the Word *and* experience. These are issues that he has personally worked through with the Lord. And in his work as a preacher, teacher, youth leader, and counselor, he has had hundreds of conversations with old and young alike who have shown him just how prevalent this problem is in our society. In fact, there seems to be no difference between race, gender, age, or even whether a person is a believer or not. Everybody faces hurts, rejections, or offenses at least one time in their lives. And most people do not know how to deal with these issues of the heart.

You may even be in a situation right now where you need to find a way out of the agony you are feeling in your heart that you don't know what to do with, or who to turn to with such deep, intimate pain. This book, of course, is not even suggesting taking the place of professional counseling, where and when such is warranted, but sometimes we may think a problem is bigger or more complicated than it really is. We should always first try taking little steps before we try to jump to the bigger ones. Even though this book may represent a "little step" to inner healing, it will definitely produce big results.

Or you may need this book just to make sure that your heart *is* clean before the Lord and that you are not robbing yourself of the blessings He wants to give you due to blockages from your side of your relationship with Him. In ridding ourselves of blockages, we will not only clean the channel between us and the Lord for our own blessings but also to be the blessing for others He has intended for us, which is where we find true fulfillment in this life.

Whatever your reason for picking up this book, I am sure you will be blessed by reading it and keeping it close by, even if only for the time in the future when you *will* be offended. As Jesus states in Luke 17:1, "It is inevitable that offenses will come...." This book helps us be prepared for just such a time as that. It will give you the necessary warfare to "Fight the good fight of faith" (2 Tim. 4:7).

Seeking together to know Him more,

Mike Bickle, Director
International House of Prayer of
Kansas City, Missouri
www.IHOP.org

Introduction

This book about the power to forgive is not theory; it is something I have painfully walked through many times. Having been sexually abused as a child, I know the hurt that comes with abuse. Having been cursed by non-Christians and well-meaning Christians, I know the struggle of battling spiritual curses. Having suffered rejection from people very close to me, I know how much we need the grace of God to forgive and move on.

But sometimes the pain is so deep it feels as if it is too hard to hold on.

I vividly remember that day when my wife and I stood in our living room trying to pray and worship the Lord. We were in the midst of one of the most devastating times of our lives. Lies about us were spreading fast throughout our country. People into whom we poured our lives suddenly rejected us and wanted no contact with us. Everything we had lived for was suddenly taken from us. Years of full-time ministry, church planting, teaching, and preaching had come to a sudden end. Close friends had become our enemies overnight. Question after question raced through my disturbed mind. *Why, Lord, why?* Heaven seemed silent. The pain was so deep; I contemplated suicide.

But as we tried to worship the Lord and pray that morning, the familiar voice of my Lord spoke to my heart. He told me that if I was willing to work through this pain—to release, forgive, and commit it all to Him—then He would use us to bring release to many Christians whom the enemy held captive through unforgiveness and bitterness. Moreover, the Lord promised that He would use these released captives as part of His end-time army to bring harm to the enemy's camp.

Suddenly everything looked different. The pain was still there, but it was all worth it. My Lord would not just help me *through* this time of trouble, but He would actually use it and allow good to come of it! Rom 8:28

We cannot be reminded enough of the importance of letting go of our past hurts and forgiving freely as we have been forgiven. A strategic plan of the enemy, however, is to bring us to a place where either we are unwilling or we believe we are unable to forgive. Satan has bound so many people simply because they are unwilling to forgive. If only these captives would realize that their freedom hinges on their choosing to forgive! If you desire (as I do) to help set these captives free—to bring healing to others through the Cross of Jesus Christ—then let us pursue God in prayer to reveal and heal our hidden hurts, failures, and mistakes.

Is 61

Therefore I present this book to you with all humility, and not with a know-it-all attitude. I simply ask you to read these pages with an open heart and mind. Allow the Spirit of God to search the depths of your being and bring to light what needs to be manifest, so that you can be released into your full potential in Christ.

All of the stories and testimonies in this book are true. In Chapter 8, the stories come from the people who experienced them. However, I have changed the names to protect the people involved. It is my hope and prayer that this book will bless you, release you, and cause you to bring release to many others.

CHAPTER 1

God's Intent

A merry heart makes a cheerful countenance, but by sorrow of the heart the spirit is broken (Proverbs 15:13).

It was fall 2001. I had just finished preaching about honoring your father and mother to thousands of spiritually hungry people in a thriving Brazilian church. As I stepped off the platform, one of the pastors brought a teenage girl to me and asked if I would minister to her. She was in her late teenage years, and her face looked aged from the emotional pain with which she had been living with since an early age. She looked pitiful. She was nothing but skin and bones. By her facial expression, I could tell that she was in deep emotional pain. As she approached me, her whole body trembled.

I asked my translator for help and listened to her story. My eyes began to fill with tears as I felt the helplessness of the situation. Could I really tell her that she needed to forgive her father and honor him? This is her story as best as I remember it.

Her father continually abused her, raping her since she was a little girl. As a young teenager, she became pregnant by him and gave birth to a daughter. The abuse continued, and now she was at a place where she could no longer live with it. She felt she had to escape. The only way she could imagine was to run away and find work to support herself. However, she knew that she would not be able to take her little daughter with her, meaning that her daughter, who was about four or five years old, would be left under the care of her father, the abuser! She was horrified at this thought, knowing that her father would then do to her daughter what he had done to her all those horrible years.

The Spirit of God deeply touched her through the message given that day. But how could she honor her father? How could she possibly forgive him when he was not even sorry for what he did and continued to do? I was fighting back the tears as I listened to her. My heart ached and tore apart as I tried to understand her heartache and confusion. She looked so helpless, lost, and confused.

As she continued to talk, my heart cried out to the Lord for help. What was I going to tell her? As my feelings and emotions went in one direction, my mind went in another. How could I possibly impart the truth to her that the Lord commands us to freely forgive as we have been forgiven? Besides all that, she had only been a Christian for a few weeks. As I kept lifting my heart to the Lord, the Spirit of God began to counsel me, and I could not help but weep with her.

Once again, I explained the importance of forgiving, telling her that the Lord does not expect her to be able to do it alone. He expects her to *make the choice*. In a vision I saw how the very Jesus who hung on a cross about 2,000 years ago and cried out to His Father to forgive His enemies, was standing right beside her offering His help. If she would be willing and obedient, His strength would come in a tangible way and enable her to do the seemingly impossible and truly forgive.

Following the prompting of the Spirit, I knelt down in front of her and as a spiritual leader and father on behalf of her abusing father, asked her to forgive me. Prompting her to verbalize forgiveness, she broke down sobbing and freely spoke out forgiveness for her father. An amazing healing power was released as I hugged her and cried with her. The Lord was truly present and faithful to His promise to help all those who call on Him. Rarely can I remember such a dramatic change in someone's countenance in just a moment. Her expression changed entirely. I have not seen her since, but pray for her often as the Spirit of God reminds me.

God's Intentions

The focus of this book is not on the wonderful effects of a merry heart, but rather on the destructive outcome of sorrow and unhealed wounds. Therefore, it is vital to understand what kind of life the Lord intends for us—for all of His children.

The Book of Proverbs tells us that a "merry heart makes a cheerful countenance." God intends for His people to be different from people who live their lives without God. From the beginning it was His desire to dwell *with* us. In the Garden of Eden, God walked and communicated with man every day. Through the death and resurrection of Jesus Christ, God does not just dwell *among* His people, but rather He *inhabits* His people. His people are now the temple of the living God in whom He lives through faith. (See Ephesians 3:17.)

God desires our hearts to be whole so that our countenance can express the amazing work of restoration that Christ brought to us through His sacrifice on the Cross. God delights in shining His wonderful light and life through ordinary people like you and me.

Throughout the Old Testament God is continually expressing His power among His people. But God does not want His power to be seen only through certain great men and women, but rather in every true Christian. Jesus stated this truth in Matthew 11:11 when He said:

> *Assuredly, I say to you, among those born of women there has not risen one greater than John the Baptist; but he who is least in the kingdom of heaven is greater than he.*

He also told His disciples that everyone who believes in Him will do greater deeds than He himself did (see John 14:12). It is important to know that God loves to show His strength through ordinary people. God wants our hearts to be whole so that we can fully enjoy the freedom from the bondages that so easily grip us. He wants our lives to radiate and express His goodness. But the devil would rather tie us up with unhealed wounds, infected by unforgiveness and bitterness, so that we will not reach our full potential.

God's Kingdom Expressed

At the end of 2004 my wife, Debi, and I took our younger son, Chris, to a local department store to buy him some clothes. While we were shopping Debi came across a pair of jogging pants she liked. As she tried them on she realized that the one pant leg was shorter than the other. She took the pants to a salesperson behind the counter, showing her the faulty pants. Debi commented that the problem might be that her legs were uneven. The woman checked the pants and told Debi that her legs were fine—the pant legs were uneven. Then the woman said, "There's nothing wrong with your legs like there is with my arms." She stretched out her arms in front of her and we were amazed by what we saw. One arm was noticeably shorter than the other.

When we asked her what happened, she told us that while she was in high school, over 20 years prior, she was on the gymnastics team. At a performance her partner was intoxicated, and at one point he was supposed to flip her, but instead he threw her across the room. The result was a long hospital stay with many surgeries due to a shattered arm and elbow. Since then her life had been one of constant pain.

Leaning over the counter, we offered her prayer, and explained to her that God is good and loves to express Himself through ordinary people. She looked around and seemed embarrassed, but agreed to let us pray for her. When Debi and I asked the Lord to show His goodness and mercy to her by healing her body, tears filled her eyes. We paid for our clothes and left, reminding her that God is good and loves to bless people.

Several months later, Debi was very excited when she returned home from shopping in town. The woman we had prayed for told Debi that she had been pain free since the day we prayed. Excitement filled my heart, and tears of joy my eyes. I realized once again that the Lord loves to express His goodness through His people.

It vital to walk the path of forgiving others and to let go of our offenses. Rather than being trapped in the pain of our past, we need to be released into the life God prepared for us, and be available to His Spirit to flow through us without hindrance.

Sorrow Breaks the Spirit

Proverbs 15:13 says:

> *A merry heart makes a cheerful countenance, but by sorrow of the heart the spirit is broken.*

Let us look at the words in the second part of Proverbs 15:13 to get a better understanding of what this Scripture really means.

> *But by the* **sorrow** *of the heart the spirit is broken.*

The Hebrew word, for *sorrow* here is the word *atstsebeth*, which means a pain or a wound. This word was also used for carving wood, when the sharp knife hit the wood and made a cut into it.

Used in this verse, it is not referring to a minor scratch or hurt, but a painful cut, which causes a wound.

Psalms 147:3 says:

*He heals the broken hearted and binds up their **wounds**.*

The very same Hebrew word, which is used in this Scripture for *wounds*, is used in Proverbs 15:13 for *sorrow*; therefore the word *sorrow* in Proverbs means wounds. There is a difference between minor scrapes and cuts and wounds. When words or actions, which others committed against us, cut deep into our hearts as the knife of the woodcarver does into the wood, we need to be aware that these wounds will not heal by themselves. If these pains are being ignored or suppressed, they will eventually become infected.

Let us look at the next word.

*By sorrow of the **heart**, the spirit is broken.*

The Hebrew word for *heart* is *leb* and has different meanings depending on the context in which it is used. Here it speaks of our soul, which is our will, mind, and emotions. We all know that pain in our soul can be very real. Wrong and hurtful words have caused very real wounds in the hearts of many.

That is why the Bible talks about emotional pain or wounds. I have heard many Christians say that emotions and feelings are something bad or irrelevant and should be ignored. If we study the Scripture, though, we will clearly see that our emotions are not just a God-given gift, but Jesus Himself expressed His emotions, both negative and positive. The Scripture records many such instances. He wept, He was angry, He was sad, He rejoiced, He loved, He grieved, He had compassion. (For instance, read John 11:35, John 2:15-17, Matthew 19:14, Mark 6:34, Matthew 23:37, Matthew 15:32, Luke 7:13, John 13:21, Mark 3:5, Mark 14:33-34, John 11:33, Mark 15:34.)

We all have been wounded in one way or another, and there are several reasons for that, which are discussed later. The fact is, wounds are inevitable. Too many people try to live their lives by building walls to protect themselves from being wounded. This is the wrong approach to life. It is far better to learn how to deal with our wounds the way the Lord wants us to deal with them than to do everything we can to avoid being wounded. It is inevitable that we will be wounded, but as we will see in a later chapter, God has provided healing for our wounds.

Samantha Made It

I remember the day clearly when I first met with Samantha. She had been carrying a hurt for many years. Growing up in a dysfunctional family where her father was a violent alcoholic, she suffered from an early age. Her parents divorced when she was young, and in her search for love, many men took advantage of her.

After she became a Christian, she just wanted to serve the Lord and follow Him wholeheartedly. Samantha forsook everything to follow the call of God on her life. She traveled to a foreign country as a missionary. But it wasn't long before she again found herself in an abusive situation. This time it was by Christian leaders who severely abused her spiritually and emotionally over a period of many years.

As we sat and talked, she told me that she would never let anyone get close to her again. She would build a wall and live behind it to be emotionally safe. This was her way of assuring that she would not get hurt anymore. My heart ached for her, as I tried to understand her pain as well as I could. I knew that wall building was not the right way to live life. I explained that if she built a wall to protect herself, she would not just keep the people out who hurt her, but also the ones who love her.

The Lord opened Samantha's eyes, and she decided not to live her life behind walls, locked away by resentment and unforgiveness. She forgave those who wounded her. With the Lord's help, she decided to make herself vulnerable again. Today, more than ten years later, Samantha is a wonderful woman of God with many friends who deeply love, respect, and appreciate her. She radiates the freedom of the Spirit and is hungry for more of Him. She made the right choice and walked through it by the grace of God.

Like Samantha, many of us have a tendency to build walls around our hearts. While healthy boundaries are like a fence that protects our heart, walls are like a prison cell in which we lock ourselves. Walls keep us from receiving all of God's gifts, as well as from giving all God wants us to give. It is important that we do not hide our pain and disappointment behind walls built around our hearts. The Kingdom of God must be received as a child. Young children normally do not have walls around their hearts.

From the very beginning God demonstrated that we are relational beings. Adam was not the one who realized that he needed a partner, but rather God said that it is not good for man to be alone (see Gen. 2:18). Only when we live freely in our God-given relationships can we fulfill our purpose and destiny. Walls around our hearts not only keep people out of our lives, but will also keep God out. He wants to touch and bless us through the people He chooses to use. Where the Spirit of the Lord is, there is freedom, (2 Cor. 3:17) but where satan operates, there is isolation (Mark 5:1-5).

A Broken Spirit

No doubt you have heard the phrase "his or her spirit is broken." People with a broken spirit are unable to reach their potential unless the Lord heals them. A broken spirit is like a ball and chain on your leg. You can be the best runner in the world, but you will never be able to successfully complete any race if you have a broken spirit.

*By sorrow of the heart **the spirit** is broken.*

The word *spirit* here is another word that is used in the Hebrew language in different ways. It is the word *ruwach*, and in this context it means life. It speaks of the energy or strength of life, which causes us to succeed in life. It is the strength that causes our lives to move forward.

The story of Joseph and his father Jacob beautifully illustrates the meaning of this word *spirit*. His brothers sold Joseph into slavery. They made his father, who loved him dearly, believe that a wild animal had killed him. His father refused to be comforted and said that he would go down to the grave to his son in mourning (see Gen. 37:31-35).

Many years later when God raised Joseph up as a ruler, his brothers had to go to Egypt to buy grain, which they needed for their survival because of a famine in the land. After a while, Joseph, whom his brothers did not recognize at first, made himself known to them. He gave them many presents and told them to bring his father to Egypt (see Gen. 45:21-28).

When Jacob heard the news that his son Joseph was alive, he regained strength. The man who could not be comforted because of the deep pain of losing his beloved son was now an old man. However, he received energy to make the long journey to Egypt. The Scripture says that his *spirit* was "revived." The Hebrew word for *spirit* in this story is the same word used in Proverbs 15:13 for *spirit*. Therefore we can see that when the Scripture says, "*...by sorrow of the heart the **spirit** is broken*," it means the strength of our life is broken.

Let's look at the last word of Proverbs 15:13.

*By sorrow of the heart the spirit is **broken.***

The word *broken* here is a strong word. It is the Hebrew word *nake* and has the meaning of being broken or stricken.

*Now the children of Judah fought against Jerusalem and took it; they **struck** it with the edge of the sword and set the city on fire* (Judges 1:8).

The word *struck* in this passage is from the same root word that Proverbs 15:13 uses for *broken*. We can see that it was not just a little pain that was caused here, but rather the destruction of a city. In the same way, if we live with deeply wounded emotions, they will lead to the destruction of our lives.

Therefore, when we live with deep, unhealed emotions rather than dealing with them the scriptural way, they will become destructive. It is not our conscious choice to live with a broken spirit, but if we choose to live with unforgiveness and bitterness, we live with sorrow of the heart, which breaks our spirit. There is no such thing as unexpressed emotions. If we suppress our pain, it will express itself in one way or another, be it through outbursts of anger, sickness, pain, compulsive behaviors, etc.

Unhealed Wounds

Over my many years in pastoral ministry, I have seen many lives destroyed because someone did not handle wounded emotions appropriately. People who live with wounded emotions will see the things that happen in their lives through their wounds. Even neutral things will look different.

We can compare this to a dog that is picked up from the pound. If the dog has been abused all of its life, no matter how much you love it, it will not be able to trust you. In fact, you may try to pet the dog, but the dog will think you are going to hurt him and snap at you. In the same way, people who live with unhealed wounds react to situations with inappropriate reactions. They will interpret the actions of others toward them through the wounds they carry inside. This is how wounds are carried into relationships.

If people do not understand this principle after going through a painful divorce or a broken relationship, they will cause themselves and others great pain. Instead of going through the right process of healing and forgiving, they enter another relationship and carry old wounds into the new relationship. Instead of finding fulfillment, they find only more pain. This can become a vicious cycle, because *hurt people hurt people.*

But I believe there is hope and healing for everyone. I trust and pray that this book will be an instrument for you and others who are on the road to healing.

When we have pain or brokenness in our hearts, it is like we are wearing dark lenses over our souls. We begin to view the world not as it is, but as we are. The darkness in our own souls reinterprets life, creating a perverted reality.[1]

The Grace of God

In his letter to Timothy, the apostle Paul told him that he persecuted the church because of his ignorance; therefore, he received the grace of our Lord. When the Lord appeared to him on the road to Damascus, he had to make a choice to stop persecuting the church and give himself wholly to the Lord. (See First Timothy 1:12-14.)

The Lord wants to heal our wounded hearts. When we first come to the Lord, we carry a lot of emotional baggage with us. The Lord graciously forgives us and imparts new life to us. He knows all the hidden areas of our hearts and the wounds that we have suppressed and ignored for various reasons. There is grace for our unhealed wounds while we are in ignorance about them. The Lord will graciously hold His protective hand over us. However, since the Lord desires to heal us, His Spirit will convict us of the unhealed areas in our lives. When He does, we must yield to Him and not put things off so as not to reject His grace.

When dealing with each other, especially with those who are still wounded, we must never forget how gracious the Lord is with us. It is important to keep our own weakness, as well as the goodness of the Lord, before our eyes. We also must be gracious with one another, just as the Lord is with us, while He works in our hearts to bring healing deliverance to us.

As we come to the end of each chapter, let's invite the Holy Spirit to search us as we check our hearts for things with which the Lord needs to deal.

ENDNOTE

1. Kris Vallotton, *Developing a Supernatural Lifestyle* (Shippensburg, PA: Destiny Image Publishers, 2007), 74.

Reality Check

What are the real dangers of unhealed wounds?

Are there obvious unhealed wounds in my life? If so, what are they?

In the past, has the Lord put his finger on wounds in my life that he wanted to heal? If so, what were they?

What is the history of dysfunctional relationships in my life?

Which fears that find entrance into my life through un-healed wounds do I struggle with frequently or have I struggled with in the past?

_____

_____

_____

_____

_____

_____

_____

_____

Prayer

My dear heavenly Father, I believe I understand the danger of living my life with a wounded heart. Please search my heart. You know me better than anyone else knows me, even better than I know myself. Let the light of Your Spirit shine upon my heart. Bring to the surface all the hidden wounds in my life. Help me face them so I can find release and healing at the Cross of Your son Jesus. Amen.

Chapter 2

Emotional Wound Causes

In this chapter we will discuss the causes of our woundedness. Knowing the causes help us to handle our pains in the right way. All of us suffer from emotional wounds. I am aware that there are countless causes; however, let's look at the most important ones.

Then He [Jesus] said to the disciples, "It is impossible that no offenses should come, but woe to him through whom they do come!" (Luke 17:1)

Reason 1. We live in a sinful world with sinful people.

No matter how nice we try to be, we all remain sinful and in need of the grace of God. Daily we have opportunities to take offense because we interact with imperfect people. Only when we have arrived in Heaven will we be interacting with perfectly holy people.

Likewise, there is no perfect church, because even if we would find it, the moment we would join it, it would no longer be perfect! Every day opportunities to take offense await us. It may be in our working environment, in busy city traffic, as we interact with our children, parents, or spouses, or in many other ways.

I remember when I boarded the plane to travel across the Atlantic. I was tired from the previous week's busy work schedule and had to fly through the night. The day of my arrival in Europe, I was already scheduled to preach. As I sat down in my assigned seat on the plane, I was hoping to get a little sleep on the long flight. After we were finally up in the air, I pushed the button to recline my seat so I could sleep. To my surprise, my seat would not recline. I pushed a little harder only to realize that there was a rather large man sitting right behind me who was pushing against my seat with his knees so that I was unable to recline it. As I looked back, he made a rude remark and assured me that he would not let me recline the seat because he needed the extra space.

Many negative thoughts shot through my head. But in the midst of trying to figure out how I would handle this situation, the Holy Spirit spoke to my heart. He reminded me that whatever I would do to sort this out, I still needed to make an important choice. Would I carry offense in my heart or would I keep my heart clean from the offense? I lifted my heart to the Lord, forgave the man, let all offense go, and also prayed the Lord's blessing over him. It was not long afterward when I was able to move to another seat where no one was behind me and I could recline my seat and get some rest.

Jesus said it is impossible that no offenses should come (see Luke 17:1). Every one of us has been hurt many times. When we see our own woundedness, it is so easy to forget that we too have often hurt other people. In this fallen, sinful world, we have become the victims of emotional pain, but we also have been the cause of emotional pain to others. Every one of us is born a sinner and in need of salvation through Jesus Christ. The Scripture makes it clear, we all have sinned.

> *But now the righteousness of God apart from the law is revealed, being witnessed by the Law and the Prophets, even the righteousness of God, through faith in Jesus Christ, to all and on all who believe. For there is no difference; for all have sinned and fall short of the glory of God* (Romans 3:21-23).

We often want to make a difference between "good" and "bad" people. However, as far as God is concerned there is no difference— all have sinned. Redemption will not be complete until we stand before the throne of God. On this earth, every one of us has to face the fact that we live in a sinful world full of sinful people. We all need to surrender ourselves to God on a daily basis. Only by His grace and the sacrifice Jesus brought through the Cross can we overcome sinfulness in our lives.

Reason 2. False expectations cause emotional wounds and offenses.

People live with expectations that are unreal, which can cause great offense in any relationship. If we have false expectations from the people to which we relate, we will get hurt and offended. If we enter marriage with expectations that are unrealistic, there will soon be offenses.

How many people have entered marriage expecting their spouse to meet all of his or her emotional needs that were not met by their own families? This is a false expectation, because only God can fully meet our emotional needs. Then, if things are left unaddressed, unforgiveness, resentment, and bitterness can creep in.

It is vital that we do not live with false expectations. We need to ask ourselves whether our expectations of people are realistic or not. Are the expectations we have of people God's plans for their lives? If we believe so, are we able to judge and interpret the plan of God for them correctly? Or are our expectations of them simply our own wishes and maybe even selfish desires? For this reason, children offend their parents and parents offend their children. Many parents have dreams for their children that are not God's plan for their lives. They get offended and hurt when their children do not fulfill their expectations. Husbands offend their wives, and wives offend their husbands. Employees offend their employers, and employers offend their employees. And so on and so on.

This is one reason why many Christians are offended by their pastors. They expect the pastor to do many things he was never called or trained to do. In their expectation, he needs to be a good worship leader, a good preacher, a good Bible teacher, a good evangelist, good at pastoral ministry, great with kids, good at administration, a great youth leader.... Because of these false expectations about pastors, people get hurt and offended. Then they blame their disappointment on the pastor without realizing that it is really their own fault.

I ministered in a church in Texas. The woman pastor told me about a man who left the church offended because he expected a man to become the new pastor, not a woman. Obviously, he had false expectations.

Reason 3. Lack of boundaries brings emotional wounds and offenses.

The subject of boundaries is a vast one, since it goes right back to an early age. Many times emotional wounds can be traced all the way to childhood, when people are the most defenseless. The heart of God grieves over the many little ones who have been hurt, wounded, and abused. His compassion goes out to such wounded people. He is full of tenderness and love, ready to heal and restore everything of which they were robbed.

Many times people have been wounded and offended because they never learned to set healthy boundaries. I won't be discussing the importance of healthy boundaries at length because others have done so excellently, especially the book *Boundaries* by Dr. Henry Cloud.[1] It is important, however, that we understand that we have full authority over our own lives. God has created us with a free will; therefore we are responsible for the choices we make. Even God never forces us to do His will. When we make the choice, for whatever reason, to allow others to step into our lives and wound us when we should have set boundaries, we are to blame.

In the Garden of Eden we can clearly see how God held everyone responsible for their own actions. Adam tried to shift the blame toward Eve and God, who had given him his wife. Eve in turn tried to shift the blame toward the serpent. God, however, declared the consequences on all three parties involved—Adam, Eve, and the serpent—thus demonstrating that everyone is responsible for their own actions and choices. (See Genesis 3:12-19.)

If we have resentment or bitterness because of other people controlling or manipulating us, we must realize that we are fully responsible for our own reactions. The Lord will be a righteous judge and judge those who have sinned against us. (See Second Corinthians 5:10.)

If we have not learned to set healthy boundaries and others wound us, we are to blame for giving up the authority God has given us over our own lives.

How many times do we say yes when we really wanted to say no? Fear of men can drive us to do that, but the Scriptures clearly show the outcome of a life lived in fear of men.

> *The fear of man brings a snare, but whoever trusts in the Lord shall be safe* (Proverbs 29:25).

Fear of men can have many reasons that might not be so obvious. It could be that we are driven to please people because we fear their anger or rejection. It might be rooted in insecurity. But whatever the root is, fear of others will cause us to be unable to set healthy boundaries. If we say yes, when we really wanted to say no, we will resent the people we said yes to when actually we are to blame. Often these people are unaware of our feelings, since they thought that we said yes from an honest heart. But we must understand that it was our dishonesty that caused the problem. We end up feeling unnecessarily hurt, offended, and used.

This is not just a theory; rather, I have lived through it painfully many times. Much of the pain I went through was because of my own insecurity—I feared the rejection of men. Driven by this insecurity I found it impossible to set boundaries, especially against people whose approval I wanted or needed. Instead of saying a wholehearted "NO," I said a gentle and shy "no," which was ignored or misunderstood and in turn caused me to comply against my own true heart's desire and went even so far as to violate my own conscience. My pain therefore was caused by others who abused me, as well as myself, who allowed the abuse.

The Vision That Changed My Life

The pain was deep and overwhelming. I thought, *Why would others do that to me? Why would others want to control and manipulate my life, causing so much pain to me and my family? Why would they use Scripture to justify their actions? Is this the end of my life, my ministry, my dreams for which I have forsaken everything?* As these and many more questions raced through my mind several years ago, I was confused and depressed. I was unable to function and needed to take time out to survive. I knew from my understanding of Scripture that I had to forgive those who hurt and wounded me. I had done so repeatedly.

Then once again the Lord spoke to my heart. He talked to me about something I did not expect to hear. He began to show me *my* role in these events.

It all came in a vision through which He clearly showed me my own sinfulness. I saw myself standing before the judgment seat of Christ. He asked me why I did certain things. Trying to excuse these actions by shifting the blame onto the Christian leaders who controlled me, the Lord made it clear that these excuses were unacceptable.

He would deal with the ones I tried to blame when they stood before Him, but now it was my turn. He then asked me why I gave up control of my life to others, when He had given me a free will and full charge of my own life. I went pale as He revealed to me that He would not accept any blame shifting.

As His question thundered through my spirit, I was speechless. Suddenly I saw that my own sin of allowing others to manipulate and control me was as evil as the sin of those who manipulated and controlled me. I repented before the Lord and asked His forgiveness.

Through this vision, I learned why I allowed others to control me, and the Lord in His grace began to work through those issues and brought healing and changes to my life. He was not condemning me, but rather leading me to repentance of my own sinfulness so that He could deal with my fear of men and insecurities—so He could make me more like Christ.

Up until that moment, I was unable to see that people can only manipulate us if we give up the control God wants us to have over our own lives. God has given us a precious gift, our free will. I found such a release when I repented, confessed this sin to God, and asked Him to forgive me for relinquishing this precious gift of my free will that He gave me.

I had plenty of excuses for why I did what I did, but in the presence of the Lord they were just explanations, because He did not accept my excuses. As we live in relationships, wounds are inevitable, but if we are wounded because we have given the control of our lives to others, we need to ask God to forgive us for doing so.

To be driven by performance orientation is an unhealthy way to live life. Instead, our relationships must be based on mutual love, respect, and acceptance. Any relationship based on performance instead of unconditional love and acceptance is an unhealthy relationship. If we need to perform in order to be accepted, we will never feel fully accepted, because we will never be able to perform "good enough," which in turn will create disappointment and wounds in our hearts.

There is a great difference between the message of the gospel and religion. Religion tries to make us perform to receive acceptance, while the gospel demonstrates that God sent His son to freely offer His love, grace, and mercy to an undeserving people. This is why the sinners loved to hang out with Jesus. The religious leaders of Jesus' time put heavy burdens on the people that they themselves were unwilling to carry. Jesus lifted the people's burdens and accepted them just as they were. (See Luke 11:46; Matthew 11:28.) God demonstrated His love for us by sending His beloved son to die for us while we were still sinners. We offer our acts of gratitude and love to God **because** He has freely accepted us and not to receive His acceptance. Our relationship with others must also be based on acceptance and not on performance.

Reason 4. Satan, the enemy of our souls, has the clear goal to destroy our lives.

Scripture clearly teaches that we have an enemy of our souls—the devil and his demons who want to destroy our lives.

Be sober, be vigilant; because your adversary the devil walks about like a roaring lion, seeking whom he may devour (1 Peter 5:8).

When satan tempted Jesus, he used Scripture. He knows the Bible. Therefore, he knows if he can cause us to live with unhealed wounds, unforgiveness, and bitterness, he can stop us from entering the purposes God has for our lives. Every one of us was created for a divine purpose. We all were created to live for something wonderful, something beyond ourselves. We will never be happy and fulfilled if we decide to live for ourselves instead of the greater purposes of God.

The Apple-Banana Demon

Although this expression is not found in Scripture, you will soon realize that you have experienced the work of this spirit in your life. Most Christians I talk to agree that they have experienced the activities of this apple-banana demon. This demon has a specific purpose—to twist words. When I say apple, he will twist the word and make it sound like banana to you. From the time the word leaves my mouth to the time it enters your ear, it sounds very different. Of course there is not a literal demon called the apple-banana demon, but this is how I classify him because it helps me to understand what is going on at times.

The enemy will do everything he can to cause confusion, misunderstanding, wounds, and offenses. Most married couples know exactly what I am talking about. How many times have I argued with my wife, assuring her that I never said what she heard? It took me a long time to understand that the enemy is active in our marriage, trying to cause misunderstanding and confusion. Once I realized this, it took a lot of pressure off of our relationship; because now he was exposed, and his plans were brought to light.

Having said this, we need to understand that there are also natural reasons why husbands and wives misunderstand each other. The way men and women communicate is very different, and it is important to make the effort to learn to understand our partners. There is enough scientific proof that the male and the female brains are wired differently to know this is true. Our own woundedness can also cause much misunderstanding when we interpret things wrongly as we read them through our pain and unhealed hearts. We need to seek the wisdom of the Lord to understand if we are just misunderstanding each other because we have not learned the art of communication, or if there is demonic activity with the goal of wounding us and destroying our relationships.

I still remember the time when I was serving as a pastor in a church that I helped plant. One time I was convinced that one of the pastors said something in his sermon that was inappropriate. When I discussed it with him, he assured me that he never said that. I was sure that he did, but he was convinced that he did not. We decided to listen to the taped message together. To my amazement, he was right. He never said it. I was very sure that he had said it. To me this was another example of the work of the apple-banana demon.

Frank and John

I have taught this important truth about how the enemy wants to use misunderstandings to cause offenses to people in the different churches I helped pastor. One Sunday morning I went to the church meeting where I was scheduled to preach. My mind was focused on the message I was about to preach in that service. Two brothers, Frank and John, were part of this church. Both were fairly new Christians and had become good friends of mine. The Lord allowed me to be part of their lives, bringing healing and restoration to them. As I entered the church building that morning, I spotted Frank at the other side of the room. It was great to see him, so I headed straight toward him. I was fully unaware that his brother John was standing right by the door. I walked right by him and did not notice him.

Immediately, different thoughts rushed through John's head as he watched me heading toward his brother. When he saw how friendly I greeted his brother, he felt offense rise up in his heart. Throughout the meeting he battled with thoughts of rejection. *What does the pastor have against me? What did I do wrong to upset him? Why does he love my brother more than me?* After the meeting, he talked to me. He told me that throughout the service he was battling with a multitude of negative thoughts, and decided to talk to me immediately. After explaining to him that I was not even aware that he was standing at the door, and that the enemy wanted to take advantage of him by causing him to be hurt, offended, and eventually bitter, he understood. Today, about 15 years later, we are still very good friends.

Do it Quickly

When taking offense, it is vital not to ignore it and let grass grow over it. John did the right thing. He did not go home with his offense and allow the enemy to fill his heart with resentment and bitterness. Instead he came to me quickly, and all things turned out well. Jesus made it clear that before we bring our gifts to Him, we need to first work things through with our offended brother.

Therefore if you bring your gift to the altar, and there remember that your brother has something against you, leave your gift there before the altar, and go your way. First be reconciled to your brother, and then come and offer your gift (Matthew 5:23-24).

We must be quick to forgive, but also quick to talk to the people we believe have offended us. Our goal must be to walk in love and unity and find reconciliation. Even if people offended us willfully and have no intentions of apologizing or asking our forgiveness, we still need to forgive them in order to not give the enemy an advantage over us. This will also help us to regain our joy and freedom in the Lord. It takes both parties to be reconciled, but only one to forgive.

ENDNOTE

1. Henry Cloud and John Townsend, *Boundaries* (Zondervan, 2002).

Reality Check

Where have I wounded other´s through my criticism?

Which of my relationships have healthy boundaries, and which don´t?

Are there people in my life with whom I still need to reconcile? If so, who are they?

Where have I fallen in the trap of the apple-banana demon? How can I change that?

Prayer

Dear heavenly Father, I understand that we live in a sinful and broken world. I realize that I was wounded many times, but I have wounded many others too. Help me to overcome all offenses in my life. Show me where I am the cause of offense to others. Give me grace to believe that You are able to use all things, even the bad things that happened to me. Show me Your ways, O Lord, and lead me on paths of everlasting life. Amen.

CHAPTER 3

Wounds vs. Scars

There is a major difference between wounds and scars. To live with unhealed wounds is a dangerous thing; however, scars are the trophies of God's grace because they show that where we once had wounds that potentially could have destroyed us, the grace of God has healed and helped us to overcome offense and bitterness.

My Personal Trophy

I carry a scar on my right upper arm. When I was a child, we had a large cherry tree in our back yard. I used to love climbing that tree. One beautiful summer day, when the cherries were ripe, my siblings and I were asked to pick them. I wanted to play outside with my friends, but my dad told me that before I could play with my friends, I had to fill my bucket a certain amount of times and take the bucket with the cherries into the kitchen. Only when I had reached my quota could I go and play with my friends.

Eager to play with my friends and facing a task that seemed too big, I decided to cheat. I climbed down off the tree before my bucket was filled and ran into the kitchen, hoping that no one would catch me. As I ran up the stairs to our front door I slipped and my right arm went through the thick glass door. Blood was everywhere, dripping from cuts on my arm. My dad quickly put pressure on the wounds to stop the heavy bleeding. I jumped into his car and held my bleeding arm out the window as he raced to the hospital, which was very close to where we lived. When I got to the hospital, the wound on my upper arm was stitched closed. The cut was less than an inch from my artery. If it would have cut that artery, I could have bled to death. I have looked at that scar many times with great thankfulness. It is a trophy of God's grace. The Lord graciously spared my life.

Likewise, our emotional scars remind us that where we were once wounded and our lives could have been destroyed, the grace of God helped us to overcome our offenses and heal our wounds, leaving scars. These emotional scars are now trophies of God's grace. There is something sweet about people who have been deeply hurt and wounded, yet allowed the Lord to deal with their wounds. There is brokenness and compassion, and the Lord delights in using such vessels. People with scars understand the wounded ones, and have a special grace to bring healing to them. In contrast, when we dress our own wounds with defensiveness, we will not learn to be ministers of His grace. Let us remember that hurt people hurt people, and healed people heal people.

Unhealed Wounds—the Great Dangers

While scars are our trophies, unhealed wounds are very dangerous. This does not only apply to individuals, but also to families, religious groups, ethnic groups, cities, and even nations.

There are nations and ethnic groups who still live with wounds that others have caused through wars, oppression, and persecution.

This can even be seen in the battle of the sexes, between males and females. If those wounds are not healed, they will become infected and cause bitterness. Infected wounds portray even neutral things as negative actions against them. Living with unhealed wounds only causes harm to one's self and not to the ones who caused the wounds. These struggles can only be defeated with repentance and true forgiveness from the heart.

Wounds Attract Flies

There are people who have no problem believing that there is a God and even angels, but when it comes to evil spirits, they want to deny their existence or at least their effectiveness. In the universe there is darkness and light. There is good and evil, devil and God, demons and angels. Since the enemy of our soul does not want our well-being and would like to hinder us from reaching our full potential for which we were created, he will either try to wound us, or stop us from getting our wounds healed.

Open wounds attract flies. In *The Types and Symbols of the Bible*, George Kirkpatrick writes that *flies* represent *evil spirits*. In the same way that unhealed physical wounds attract *flies*, unhealed emotional wounds attract *evil spirits*.

Jesus called satan the father of lies; therefore, the natural thing for him to do is to lie. (See John 8:44.) Since he is the father of lies, his evil spirits are good at lying too. Truth will set us free, but lies will keep us in bondage. We must expose lies and live in the truth, which of course is Jesus Himself.

It is vital for us to understand that unforgiveness is sin, and sin is of the realm of darkness. Demonic spirits can attach themselves to our unhealed wounds, because these wounds are rooted in our unforgiveness. If we ignore our knowledge of Scripture and the prompting of the Holy Spirit and refuse to forgive, we decide to keep a part of our lives in darkness, which is the realm of the devil and his evil spirits.

Using our authority as believers to cast out these evil spirits will not do the job. Those spirits have legal access to our lives because of the open door of unforgiveness. In order to be free, we must first close the door by letting go of all offense, releasing all unforgiveness to the Lord, and forgiving those who have wounded us. Then we can exercise our God-given authority and the enemy will have no choice but to flee from us and stay away.

Many years ago I was disturbed by the lack of lasting results in the lives of believers receiving deliverance ministry. I set time aside to seek the Lord to effectively help the struggling believers. I wanted to know how people could be delivered from demonic oppression and remain free. One night the Lord spoke to me through a dream in which it became clear that if we do not first remove the issues in our lives that give demonic forces a legal right in our lives, there can be no lasting freedom.

> But He gives more grace. Therefore He says: "God resists the proud, But gives grace to the humble." Therefore submit to God. Resist the devil and he will flee from you (James 4:6-7).

I have heard many well-meaning Christians quote this Scripture partially. It is not enough to resist the devil; we must first walk in humility and submit to God. We will only have authority over the enemy in our lives in the areas that we have submitted to God. If we refuse to obey God in the area of finances and the enemy constantly attacks this area of our lives, the solution is not to rebuke him, but rather to submit this area to God, then rebuke him and he will flee from us. God will not change His laws to fit our lives; we must adapt our lives to the laws of His Kingdom.

Fear—a Destructive Force

Fear is a strong emotion. There are many references in the Bible that command us not to live our lives in fear. (See Joshua 1:9; Joshua 8:1; Judges 6:10; Psalms 91:5; Proverbs 3:25; Isaiah 43:1; Isaiah 44:8; Matthew 10:26; Hebrews 13:6.) There are healthy and protective fears, such as not going too close to the edge of a cliff because we are afraid of falling down and dying. However, there are fears that cripple our lives and hold us back from fulfilling our God-given purpose in life. If we look back, everyone can remember incidents in which fear crippled us. We did not do the things we really wanted to do, and maybe even should have done, simply because fear held us back.

One way these fears can find an open door in our lives is through unhealed wounds. Fighting these fears isn't the right approach; we must get to the very root of the fear. If fears find entrance into our lives through unhealed wounds, we must receive healing for those wounds, which will close the door to fear. I am aware that not every fear is caused by unhealed wounds; however, we must allow the Holy Spirit to search our hearts and go to the root of our problems.

Offense—the Power Killer

When Jesus lived on earth, He did great and astonishing miracles. People flocked to Him because they knew that He would meet their needs. He willingly healed their sicknesses and diseases; He even raised the dead. When He taught, He did so with authority, passion, and compassion. But there was one place, His own hometown, where He was unable to perform great miracles. There He only laid hands on a few sick and healed them.

How could this be, that the very son of God who moved in such amazing power was unable to perform great miracles in Nazareth? What hindered the power of God? Scripture tells us that when He came to His hometown, people were astonished at the great miracles He had performed. However, they also took offense. They said, *"...is this not the carpenter, the Son of Mary, and brother of James, Joses, Judas, and Simon? And are not His sisters here with us?' So they were offended at Him..."* (Mark 6:1-5).

It was their offense that caused them to walk in unbelief and neutralized His power that was available to them. As it was with the people in Jesus' hometown, so it is often with us. It is not that other people offend us, but rather we are taking offense from what people say or do.

Let us look at another great story that illustrates this point so well.

> *Then Jesus went out from there and departed to the region of Tyre and Sidon.*
>
> *And behold, a woman of Canaan came from that region and cried out to Him, saying, "Have mercy on me, O Lord, Son of David! My daughter is severely demon-possessed." But He answered her not a word. And His disciples came and urged Him, saying, "Send her away, for she cries out after us." But He answered and said, "I was not sent except to the lost sheep of the house of Israel." Then she came and worshiped Him, saying, "Lord, help me!" But He answered and said, "It is not good to take the children's bread and throw it to the little dogs." And she said, "Yes, Lord, yet even the little dogs eat the crumbs which fall from their masters' table." Then Jesus answered and said to her, "O woman, great is your faith! Let it be to you as you desire." And her daughter was healed from that very hour* (Matthew 15:21-28).

In this story the woman had opportunity to get offended with Jesus. After all He initially refused to help her and seemed even rude to her. But instead of taking offense, she kept pursuing the love and power of God and received her miracle.

It is God's divine plan to use people to minister His grace to others. Offense will hinder us from receiving from the people who offended us, because we no longer can see these people the way they really are. God might have chosen to use these very people to minister His grace gifts to us, but we will see them through the glasses of our offense. This offense will blur our vision and cause us to stop the power of God from flowing through them toward us. It is vital for us to understand that it is the Lord who chooses the channels He uses. Therefore we must rid our hearts from all offenses to be able to receive everything the Lord has for us from anyone.

Closing the Door

The enemy of our soul will try to intimidate us with his lies. However, there is a difference when he just comes and lies to us, or when his lies find entrance into our wounded hearts. He is the father of all lies, and lying is part of his nature. When our wounded hearts attract these lies, they are overwhelming. No matter how much we try to resist or overcome them, they will return because our unhealed wounds are open doors for his lies. It makes no sense to try to throw an intruder out of the house if we leave the doors wide open for him to come right back in. The logical thing to do would be to throw him out of the house and make sure that all entryways are securely shut. Only then can we find safety. When our wounded hearts are open doors for the enemy we must make sure that we allow the Lord to heal those wounds, to find true freedom and safety. If wounded hearts open the door to the enemy, then healed hearts will be closed doors to the enemy.

Infected Wounds

As it is in the natural, so it is in the spiritual. If we ignore open wounds, there is a great danger that they will become infected. Every mother knows that when her children hurt themselves and have wounds that are bleeding, they must not be ignored. If there is dirt in the wound the wound must be cleaned and protected in order to heal and not become infected.

When I was growing up, we used natural remedies. There is a plant that grows on the mountains of Austria called Arnica. This particular plant is used for a variety of remedies, and is known as a good natural disinfectant. The plants were picked, put in a bottle, and mixed with rubbing alcohol. After awhile it was filtered, leaving a little bottle with a wonderful reddish brown liquid.

There were plenty of wounds in our family because my mom had ten kids, and six were boys. We did not have a television or video games, so therefore we spent most of our time outside. When someone got hurt, the bottle of Arnica with alcohol was brought out, and Mom applied it to the wound. It burned like fire and was not pleasant at all, but Mom told us plenty of times how important it was to make sure the wound did not get infected.

I still remember the day my brother and I fought over the metal poker that we used to stoke the furnace. Both of us wanted it and struggled fiercely for it. I refused to let go, and as he pulled it toward him, it cut my lower arm.

Because I didn't want Mom to put Arnica in the open wound because it burned so badly, I ignored it and hid it from her. It was not long until the wound was infected. There was a visible line going up my arm. It was growing fast and was already near my shoulder. Dad was gone on some preaching trip, and Mom was busy with her eight children all by herself, which made it easier for me to hide my wound. I wore only long sleeves and hoped that Mom wouldn't notice. But someone told her about it, and when she saw it, she immediately took me to the hospital. The doctor said I had blood poisoning—the wound was infected and had to be treated quickly and appropriately, otherwise it would cause dangerous health problems. The doctor cleaned the wound, and for several days I received shots of antibiotics. I learned that if wounds were ignored and not dealt with appropriately, they do not just remain harmless wounds, but instead become a dangerous progression of ill health.

Dangerous Progression

If we ignore our emotional wounds, they will progress to unforgiveness, resentment, the desire for revenge, bitterness, and eventually hatred that will cause us to actually take revenge. It is important that we do not ignore our wounds but rather stop the dangerous progression as soon as possible. If we refuse to forgive those who wounded us, this dangerous progression will accelerate.

Resentment

When we do not forgive those who wounded us, our unforgiveness will progress to resentfulness. We will not resent only the people who hurt us; we will begin to resent others too because of our unresolved and unhealthy emotional memories. When we begin to interact with people who subconsciously remind us of the people we resent, we will feel resentment toward those people although they have done nothing to us.

This is a destructive force in relationships. How can we live or work together with people we resent? There will be no honesty and openness in these relationships. We will be unable to receive anything from people we resent, even if they would want to bless us and do us good. If we live with resentment in our hearts, we can run as far as we want to, but we will never outrun our problem of resentment. There will always be people who remind us of the people we resent. At times the Lord will intentionally bring these people into our lives so we can fully surrender our wounded hearts to Him and find freedom and healing. Since we cannot outrun our problems, we might as well face them, deal with them, and allow the Lord to use them for His and our good.

Desire for Revenge

If unforgiveness has progressed to resentment and we still refuse to deal with our wounds in the right way, the progression will continue. Resentment will turn into the desire for revenge. I do not believe that the desire for revenge is motivated by bitterness. *Taking* revenge is, but the *desire* for revenge is just another step in the progression toward self-destruction. This desire cannot be gratified. Because its motivation is unforgiveness and resentment, it is an impure motivation, which only brings bitter fruit into our lives.

If we realize that there are desires and thoughts to take revenge, we must understand that these desires are unquenchable. We must take actions to stop further progression. The steps we need to take are discussed in the following chapters. The sooner we begin the right steps, the easier they will be. Often it is our attitude that keeps us trapped. We are made to believe that it is an impossible task to face our pain. But once we change our attitude and make the decision to deal with it, the hardest part is accomplished.

If we do not deal with our desire for revenge, it can lead us to taking revenge. There is a major difference between restitution and revenge. We need to appeal our cases to higher authorities to receive justice. We, who have been hurt, are not able to judge the correct restitution.

> *Beloved, do not avenge yourselves, but rather give place to wrath; for it is written, "Vengeance is Mine, I will repay," says the Lord* (Romans 12:19).

When we are hurt, abused, and wounded, we need to understand that God Himself is on the side of the weak and wounded. We need to allow the Lord to take care of us and be our defender. He can judge correctly with no bitterness, defiled vision, or partiality. We need to be thankful that we live in a country where we have a justice system. I am aware that it does not always operate justly, because it is comprised of humans who are fallible; nevertheless, our God sits on the throne and He is well-able to override every human authority to make sure we get justice.

Once we come to the place where we have decided to take revenge, the bitterness that has defiled us will be the motivating force. Even if we believe that we can see clearly, we can not. Bitterness dims our vision; therefore, Scripture commands us to leave vengeance to Him. Let us not do what a dear Christian brother said to me once, when he tried to get his rights. After I told him that the Scripture teaches that we should leave vengeance to the Lord, he replied: "Yes, but the Lord uses people, and this time he has chosen to use me."

Bitterness

If the progression has not been halted up to this point, the next step is bitterness. It is dangerous to live our lives in bitterness. The gifts the Lord has placed within us will not cease to function just because we are bitter.

> *For the gifts and the calling of God are irrevocable* (Romans 11:29).

However, these gifts will be flowing through an unclean channel. We will be mixing the pure with the unclean. You can have the purest of all waters, but if your water pipes and your faucets are contaminated with all sorts of filth, the water will be undrinkable; it could even be dangerous to drink. Once we have progressed to this stage it is not just a problem of our own, but now it will affect others. No matter how pure the *source* is, if the *channel* is unclean it will affect those who are thirsty and want to drink from the fountain of living water that the Lord has placed within us. The Bible clearly warns us to be ruthless toward bitterness.

The writer to the Hebrews admonishes Christians to pursue peace with all.

> *Pursue peace with all people, and holiness, without which no one will see the Lord: looking carefully lest anyone fall short of the grace of God; lest any root of bitterness springing up cause trouble, and by this many become defiled;* (Hebrews 12:14-15).

Notice that he tells us to *pursue* peace with all people. There will always be people who are unwilling to live in peace with us, but that is not our responsibility. Our task is to *pursue peace*. We cannot pursue peace if our hearts are filled with bitterness. Bitterness brings strife and war, not peace.

As the writer talks about pursuing peace with all people, he also admonishes us to *look carefully* for roots of bitterness. In our pursuit of peace, there will always be opportunities to become bitter. There will always be people who will refuse to live in peace; as discussed in an earlier chapter, we live in a sinful world with sinful people.

Not Just Our Private Problem

We are not just to glance at our hearts to see if there are any roots of bitterness; rather, we are to look carefully. Why is this so important? Because bitterness is not a problem that concerns only us, it affects many. Having been involved in church planting and pastoral ministry for years, I have seen many times how bitterness can permeate. Good people have been terribly hurt. Instead of dealing with wounds the right way, they refuse to forgive, and the path to destruction begins. Before long they become bitter people.

As born-again Christians, they are part of the Body of Christ, which is not an organization but a living organism. Therefore their bitterness spreads and has the potential to poison others, much like cancer cells take over, destroy, and deform good, healthy cells. We do not help people who have become bitter by just sitting and listening to them. This only causes us to become trash cans for their bitterness. The root of bitterness has the potential to defile many, as the writer of the Book of Hebrews clearly states: "...*lest any root of bitterness springing up cause trouble, and by this many become defiled*" (Hebrews 12:15).

Our hearts must be touched by the needs of others, but it is a false and impure compassion if we just listen to others in their bitterness. Rather, with humility and hearts filled with compassion and mercy, we need to lead them to look closely at their hearts and bring them to a place of repentance so they can be released from their bitterness, find healing, and bring healing to others.

Hurt people will hurt people. The word *defile* in the Hebrews' passage means "to contaminate." Bitterness will contaminate us and others. I have been guilty of carrying bitterness in my heart, and I am glad that there is forgiveness for my sins. I have asked the Lord in repentance to heal and release all the people whom I have contaminated with my bitterness. He will do the same for you when you ask.

Hatred

When we have progressed to the hatred stage, we are in great danger. Hatred needs an outlet. The Scripture has some strong warnings about being hateful. When the news reports a terrible and seemingly unpredictable crime, people are shocked. We wonder: *How can someone who seemed so quiet and introverted take a gun and shoot innocent people? How can terrorists kill themselves in order to kill others whom they hate? How can this be? How can people be so horrible?*

Nobody is exempt from committing atrocities. History shows us that more than one religious group is capable of committing such acts. Look what happened during the crusades. Often expressed hatred has its origin in unhealed wounds. People who live with unhealed wounds progress up the ladder of destruction until hatred fills their hearts. Because hatred needs an outlet, it finds one in revenge. Wounded people blame others for their misfortune. But in reality they live out their hatred as they wound others, because hurt people hurt people and healed people heal people.

Please note that I do not by any means justify those actions; rather, I am trying to explain them. If we refuse to allow the Lord to heal our wounds and live a life of unforgiveness, we are all capable of climbing the ladder of destruction that begins from being wounded and not forgiving, becoming resentful, to desiring for revenge, to bitterness, to hating and actually taking revenge.

The Scripture has clear warnings about hatred.

Whoever hates his brother is a murderer, and you know that no murderer has eternal life abiding in him (1 John 3:15).

If someone says, "I love God," and hates his brother, he is a liar; for he who does not love his brother whom he has seen, how can he love God whom he has not seen? (1 John 4:20)

Reality Check

Which infected wounds in my heart am I aware of?

Have I progressed up the ladder of dangerous destruction? If so, how far am I?

Where can I detect bitterness in my life?

Where am I in danger of listening to the bitterness of others, and when have I infected others with my bitterness?

Prayer

Dear Father in Heaven. I thank You that You are full of mercy and the God of all grace. I ask You today to give me grace so I can be healed. By Your Holy Spirit, show me my heart the way You see it. I want to become whole and free. Bring to light everything that displeases You and help me on the road to healing. Help me not to take offense so I can close all doors to the enemy. I trust you that you will lead me in the right direction. Amen.

CHAPTER 4

Steps to Healing

Can everyone receive healing from emotional wounds and pain? The answer: yes! No matter how deep the pain is, there is healing available for everyone. However, healing will not take place just because we say the right prayer or go to counseling or therapy. These things are good, but there are steps we need to take to find healing and release from our emotional pain. Discussed in this chapter is the importance of taking the right steps, rather than racing through shortcuts. Specific steps are discussed in detail in the following chapters.

We often want to take shortcuts in our lives—especially when it comes to emotional healing. If therapy or counseling only gets us to understand why we have been hurt and whose fault it is, as therapy alone often does, it will not bring us to a place of total healing.

Oftentimes it makes us feel better when we are able to talk about our pain; however, this is only temporary relief. It is good to find people who can empathize with us, but if we are unwilling to walk through the process of healing, we will not become the whole person God has created.

For instance, you go to the doctor because of a pain in your abdomen. After an examination and tests, the doctor says that you have colon cancer. He says that you need surgery and other treatments in order to be healed. When you leave his office you are devastated by the prognosis. At home you call several of your friends and share the bad news. They listen to you, comfort you, cry with you, and encourage you. You feel a little better, but the problem is not solved. For you to become healthy, you have to follow the steps the doctor prescribed for you.

In the same way, we need to walk through the necessary steps God shows us in order to receive healing for our wounded hearts. There are no shortcuts, but if we are willing to walk through the steps, there is healing and release.

The Great Misconception—Time Heals Wounds

How many times have well-meaning people told others with emotional wounds just to be patient because "time heals all wounds"? While it does take time to heal wounds, time itself does not heal them. There is a major difference between whether *time heals wounds or it takes time to heal wounds.*

Imagine going to the hospital because you think you have a broken leg. After X-rays were taken and you were examined, the doctor says that the leg needs to be in a cast, which will stay on your leg for six weeks. You assure the doctor that you understand the healing process—time will heal your leg. In six weeks, your leg will be healed.

If you get up and leave the hospital without a cast because you believe that *time* will heal your leg, you will have a rude awakening.

Yes, it takes time to heal your leg, but time itself does not heal it. If you continue to walk around on your broken leg, even though the fracture would grow together, it will grow together crooked and you will have damaged your leg rather than healed it.

Wounds need to be examined and identified correctly, and then the person needs to take the right steps to ensure total and appropriate healing.

Taking the Right Steps

We live in a fast-paced world where immediate results are expected. Daily the media informs us about the many things we *need*. Sometimes we can even wonder how we survived so far without so much we are obviously "missing." Countless times we are being told that without all the different things offered to us, we cannot live happily or be satisfied.

The problem is not all the new and wonderful things. The problem is that we are made to believe we must have them immediately. We're told that we do not need to save the money to buy what we would like to have. Instead, we can make a simple phone call, provide our credit card number, and within days, we receive the "needed" item. If our credit card is maxed out, we simply use the other cards we carry in our wallets. If we need a new car, no problem, we just drive it home and pay for it later. Why save and wait for what we want? After all, our society believes in instant gratification. Remember, though, the really valuable things take time to acquire. We need to understand that nothing of worth comes quickly.

One beautiful sunny afternoon I took my older son Danny for a walk. At that time he was preschool age, and he began talking to me about a certain toy that he "needed" so badly. He pleaded with me to buy it for him. As I tried to explain to him that the first step is to save up enough money to buy it, then we could go buy it, he looked stunned. He said there was no need to do that. "Daddy, just stick the plastic card in the machine, and you will get money," he told me. I had to teach him that there are steps to take to be able to "stick the plastic card in the machine" and get money. First, you must work hard to earn the money. Then you must put the money into the bank. Once you have done that, you can take it out through the machine.

Likewise, it is vital to understand that our healing does not happen instantly just because we want it to. The Lord is well-able to do anything and can heal us in a moment of time. But He has chosen for us to live our lives here on earth, constantly and earnestly seeking Him. Therefore, if we are willing to walk through the right steps and keep pace with the Lord, He will meet us as we walk the path toward our healing.

People would like to win the prize without running the race. There are many who want to receive the reward without having to work hard for it. Many would like to be overcomers without having to face the struggles and hardships to overcome.

I remember when my brother, who used to be overweight, decided that it was time to change his lifestyle. As a child he was rather easy going. I remember my frustration whenever he played soccer with us. Running after the ball was not on his agenda. Should the ball happen to come his way, he would be willing to kick it. One day, many years later, he realized that change was necessary if he wanted to remain healthy. He began to get serious. He exercised regularly over a long period of time, lost a lot of weight, felt great, and decided to run a marathon.

With time and hard work his success came, and he truly ran a marathon successfully. Now that he got a taste of how good it felt to be fit, he decided to run a marathon under three hours. He worked extremely hard, continually put his body under subjection, and practiced tirelessly. Sure enough, the day came when he ran the marathon under three hours. Meanwhile, he even successfully completed an iron man event. It took many small steps, hundreds of days of practice, and overcoming laziness to reach his goal.

My other brother was inspired and began to practice for a marathon too. He never had the goal to run the marathon under three hours, but sure enough, he completed the marathon in less than four hours. Now it was my turn. My brothers encouraged me to run a marathon as well. I have never been a long-distance runner, although I always liked sports. I asked my brother who ran the marathon under three hours to put together a training plan so I could work toward my goal of running through the finish line of the Vienna City Marathon.

As I read the plan he sent me and studied it thoroughly, I realized that I would be unable to run a marathon unless I practiced hard for a long time. It would take specific steps followed in a specific way to be successful. I wanted to run the race, but I did not want to take the steps necessary to be successful. Guess what? To this day I have never run in a marathon. I didn't have the patience or the strong desire to make it happen.

Similarly, many want to inherit God's promises with only faith instead of faith *and* patience. Although I am thankful for the faith movement that has taught us so much in regard to trusting God to receive our promises, I have considered starting a patience movement, since it is by faith *and patience* that we inherit His promises.

> *For God is not unjust to forget your work and labor of love which you have shown toward His name, in that you have ministered to the saints, and do minister. And we desire that each one of you show the same diligence to the full assurance of hope until the end, that you do not become sluggish, but imitate those who through faith and patience inherit the promises* (Hebrews 6:10-12).

We must endure to the end, keep trusting the Lord for our healing, and have patience as we take the necessary steps to healing.

Recently I spoke with Amanda, a dear woman in a European country where I have ministered many times. I have been praying for her for several years. She is not well—emotionally disturbed, troubled by nightmares, and thoughts of suicide. She has been in this struggle for many years. She really loves the Lord, but seems unable to find a way out of her haunting situation. Over the past years, she was placed in a psychiatric hospital several times where she was treated with medication, but with no success. As we talked on the phone, I advised her to get help from a good Christian counselor, with whom I was acquainted. I reminded her that Jesus was her only answer; however, He often uses people to help us come to healing and wholeness.

I assured her that this counselor loved the Lord and ministered to people with great understanding and compassion. Amanda's answer astounded me. Someone had already recommended that particular Christian ministry to her, but said there was a waiting list up to two or three months for an appointment. Therefore she put the idea aside. I reminded her that she had been struggling for almost 20 years, and three months was a short time compared to the long time she had been suffering. I encouraged her to take the necessary steps to become whole and well. Many people have prayed for her healing and expected an instant miracle. Yes, our God does do instant miracles, and I have witnessed them many times myself. But often, for various reasons we might not understand, our Lord would have us walk through the process and take the right steps to find healing and release.

Reality Check

Which wounds in my heart have I ignored, because I am unwilling to take time for my healing?

_____

_____

_____

_____

_____

_____

_____

In which areas does my impatience hinder me from receiving my healing?

Where have I judged others or put pressure on them because they are not as far as I expect them to be in their healing process?

Prayer

Dear Father in Heaven, thank You that nothing is impossible for You. Thank You that You are a God who cares for me. Please help me to take the right steps. Help me in my impatience. Help me to endure. You know all things. You know which steps I need to take at which time in order to receive healing and wholeness. Please lead me the right way. I am willing to walk Your way and take Your steps. Amen.

CHAPTER 5

Step 1—Repentance

The obvious question that comes to mind when we talk about this first step on the path to our healing is why we who were wounded, hurt, and abused should have to repent. Aren't the people who hurt us the ones who need to repent?

What Is Repentance?

Let's first consider what biblical repentance means—it means to change your mind or to turn around. There is a difference between saying, "I am sorry," and truly repenting. We can be sorry for what we have done for many reasons. We might be sorry because we were caught and now have to face the consequences. Maybe we are sorry because we live with a desire to be accepted by others and now we fear rejection because of our actions.

I was on my way to the south of Austria to teach, preach, and spend a few days with one of the churches we had planted. Needing a new pair of pants, I decided to stop about halfway where I knew a department store was having a sale. Outside the store were parking spaces for which one had to pay; however, there were also free ten-minute spaces. Being sure that it would take me no more than 10 minutes to pick a pair of pants, I decided to park without paying. In no time, I found pants that were on sale, tried them on, and went to the checkout area, excited that I saved about $30.

There was only one checkout lane open, and the woman in front of me had some time-consuming problems—more time than I had. By the time I finally got back to my car, I had been gone for just a little over the allowed 10 minutes. To my despair, I saw a parking ticket on my windshield. Since the police officer was still in sight, I talked to her, trying to explain the situation. She made it clear to me that I had to pay a $30 fine, even though I had only parked for two extra minutes.

As I drove off complaining to myself about the police officer and the woman in the store, I was feeling sorry for myself about having to pay the parking ticket, which meant that in the end I had not saved any money on the sale. About that time, the Holy Spirit brought conviction to my heart. He asked me why I was so sorry about the $30. I was sorry that I had to pay the ticket—but not at all sorry that I broke the law. I was sorry, but for the wrong reason.

It is appropriate to feel sorry and feel remorse and conviction, but if it does not lead to repentance, it has not achieved its purpose. We may take a wrong turn by mistake and end up driving our car the wrong way on a one-way street. Once we realize what we have done, it is not enough to be sorry; we need to turn around so not to endanger others and ourselves. Repentance means turning around and changing direction. As faith without works is dead faith, so repentance without fruit is dead repentance.

Fruit of Repentance

John the Baptist baptized the people with a baptism of repentance. Many people came to him to be baptized and confess their sins. The religious leaders also came to him to be baptized. His response to them was very brutal. Unlike some of today's reactions, he did not get excited when the leaders showed up and quickly counted the numbers so that he could announce how successful his ministry was. He also did not try to keep them happy so they would join him. He called them a "brood of vipers!" So much for being seeker friendly! John knew that some outward action and ritual alone would not do the job. He told them clearly that they had to bring fruit of repentance to show that their repentance was genuine.

> *But when he saw many of the Pharisees and Sadducees coming to his baptism, he said to them, "Brood of vipers!"* (Matthew 3:7)

Repentance is more than words; it is action. It means changing our minds and then doing something about it. Repentance is the first important step leading to our healing and wholeness because it strengthens us to overcome unforgiveness and bitterness.

If we struggle with unhealed wounds, resentment, and bitterness, it is because we have held on to it and not brought it to the Lord. Maybe we never made the conscious choice to hold on to our wounds and bitterness, but the choice not to bring it to the Lord equals the choice to hold on to it. To hold on to unforgiveness and bitterness, for whatever reason, is sin. The topic of unforgiveness is discussed more in the next chapter.

Repenting From Our Unforgiveness

To begin the healing process, we need to repent of all the grudges we hold toward other people. We do not need to repent for what others have done to us, or the pain that others have caused us to feel, but we do need to repent for holding on to our pain and not forgiving them freely.

I understand that it is easy to believe that we have a right to hold on to our unforgiveness when we are so deeply wounded, but that is not the truth. Unless we are willing to first see our own sin of unforgiveness and repent from it, we cannot continue on the road to wholeness. I want to emphasize here that we do not repent for any actions committed against us, but only for *our response* to those actions. Anytime we hold on to our wounds instead of releasing them to the Lord, we need to repent for it. Anytime we harbor unforgiveness and bitterness toward people who have abused us, we need to repent for *our response* to the sin committed against us.

Repenting From Our Blame Shifting

Blame shifting will keep us from repenting. Blame shifting started in the Garden of Eden. Adam blamed Eve and God by telling God that it was the woman that He created that caused him to sin. Eve in turn blamed the serpent.

Both Adam and Eve tried to avoid responsibility for their actions. The Lord declared the consequences to all parties involved, to the man, the woman, and the serpent. Everyone was held responsible for his or her own actions.

Then the Lord God called to Adam and said to him, "Where are you?" So he said, "I heard Your voice in the garden, and I was afraid because I was naked; and I hid myself." And He said, "Who told you that you were naked? Have you eaten from the tree of which I commanded you that you should not eat?" Then the man said, "The woman whom You gave to be with me, she gave me of the tree, and I ate." And the Lord God said to the woman, "What is this you have done?"

The woman said, "The serpent deceived me, and I ate." So the Lord God said to the serpent: "Because you have done this, you are cursed more than all cattle, and more than every beast of the field; on your belly you shall go, and you shall eat dust all the days of your life. And I will put enmity between you and the woman, and between your seed and her Seed; He shall bruise your head, and you shall bruise His heel."

To the woman He said: "I will greatly multiply your sorrow and your conception; In pain you shall bring forth children; your desire shall be for your husband, And he shall rule over you." Then to Adam He said, "Because you have heeded the voice of your wife, and have eaten from the tree of which I commanded you, saying, 'You shall not eat of it': "Cursed is the ground for your sake; in toil you shall eat of it all the days of your life. Both thorns and thistles it shall bring forth for you, and you shall eat the herb of the field. In the sweat of your face you shall eat bread till you return to the ground, for out of it you were taken; for dust you are, and to dust you shall return" (Genesis 3:9-19).

Repenting From Our Bitterness

If we are not ruthless about ridding the bitterness, this poison will affect all areas of our lives. There is no other way to deal with it but to truly repent before the Lord.

Bitterness is a result of our unforgiveness and is often hard to deal with, because it is easy to believe that we have a right to hold on to it. It is one thing to be wounded by people, but it is another thing altogether to allow these wounds to progress to bitterness.

If we continue to live in our bitterness, we will isolate ourselves from healthy relationships. Since the root of bitterness poisons other people as well, healthy people who do not want to become bitter people will avoid being in a relationship with us. Soon the only friends we will have will be other bitter people.

Repenting From Our Resentment Toward God

On top of the bitterness and resentment we can carry toward others and ourselves, we can also be resentful and bitter toward God. Usually the reason for our bitterness toward God has nothing to do with what He has done to us. It has to do with our misunderstanding or wrong perception of God and His nature, and what we perceive He has done to us.

There may be various reasons why our perception of God is unreal. However, if we hold any resentment or bitterness toward God, we must let it go. Often when we reap the consequences of our own wrong choices, we feel tempted to blame God. It is vital for us to understand God's true nature of love.

Understanding the Discipline of God

How can we receive healing and release from our wounds if we carry offense against the God who wants to heal us? We will be unable to come to Him with open hearts and receive His gifts of mercy and grace. It is important to understand the discipline of God, in order to release our resentments against Him. If we do not have a right understanding of God's discipline, we will not be able to embrace it, which is an important aspect in our spiritual maturity. Since God's discipline is part of all of His children's lives, we will either embrace it or resent it. A misunderstanding of the nature of God's discipline can be the cause of resentment toward Him.

The Scripture speaks clearly about God's discipline toward his children. (See Hebrews 12:4-11.)

God never disciplines us for our harm or because He is angry with us. To understand this we must look at different aspects in this passage in Hebrews. First, we must see the *motive* of God in His discipline toward us. Then we must see the meaning in the different words used for *discipline*.

> *Furthermore, we have had human fathers who corrected us, and we paid them respect. Shall we not much more readily be in subjection to the Father of spirits and live? For they indeed for a few days chastened us as seemed best to them, but He for our profit, that we may be partakers of His holiness* (Hebrews 12:9-10).

The writer of the Book of Hebrews makes a comparison between our natural fathers and our heavenly Father. No matter how godly our natural fathers were, they still only disciplined us as seemed best to *them*. Our heavenly Father, however, always disciplines us *for our own profit*, that we may be partakers of His holiness.

There is no selfish or earthly motive in our heavenly Father's discipline toward us. It is all for our good. God will never discipline us because we irritate Him, get on His nerves, or embarrass Him, but only for our own good.

Progressive Discipline

There is a progression of discipline that our heavenly Father uses—chastening, rebuking, and scourging. Notice these three words in the following passage:

> *And you have forgotten the exhortation which speaks to you as to sons: "My son, do not despise the* **chastening** *of the Lord, nor be discouraged when you are* **rebuked** *by Him; for whom the Lord loves He chastens, and* **scourges** *every son whom He receives* (Hebrews 12:5-6).

First, the Lord *chastens* us, then He *rebukes* us, and then He *scourges* us. These three words, which all have a different meaning, are used in this progressive order.

Here we can see the pattern God uses with His children. The Greek word for *chastening* is the word *paideia*, which means to teach, instruct, or train.[1] In his love, the Lord will teach and instruct us in the ways we need to walk. He will do this through various means. He may use the Bible, books, sermons, prophetic words, and many other ways in which He teaches and instructs us how to live our lives.

If we, in our own folly, decide to reject the instruction of the Lord, He moves to the second way of disciplining us—rebuking. The Greek word used in this passage for *rebuke* is the word *elegcho*, which means to rebuke, to convict, to uncover, to bring into the light.[2] It is the desire of the Lord that all of His children respond to His instruction. Because the Lord loves us enough and does not want us to walk toward our own self-destruction, He will use the next level of discipline, which is to convict us and bring things to light in order for us to see them and repent of them. Hopefully by this time we have repented before the Lord, humbled ourselves, and turned from our wrong ways or actions. If necessary, the Lord will take the next step in the process of disciplining His children. The Greek word for *scourging* in this passage is *mastigoo*. In the New Testament, it is without exception used as a physical punishment.

It is vital for us to understand that the Lord in His love will not just beat us over the head. People harbor resentment against the Lord because they blame Him for pain and hardship in their lives, which He has never caused.

The Lord will discipline His children, but He will only do it out of the pure motive of love, because God is love. He will always first instruct and teach us. If we are willing and obedient and respond to the Lord's instruction, we do not have to face the rebuke, conviction, and scourging of the Lord.

Therefore we must release any resentment against God. Even if we have faced His severe discipline, it is only because we have not responded to Him when He instructed us. We must never avoid the discipline of the Lord but always submit to it. As long as the Lord disciplines us, He has not given up on us. Once we are beyond the Lord's discipline, we are in danger.

Repentance—at the Beginning and the End

At the very beginning of the New Testament church after the Holy Spirit was poured out on the day of Pentecost and Peter preached a very convicting sermon, he admonished the people to repent. In fact, when the people asked Peter what they must do in order to be saved, the first thing Peter told them to do was repent.

> *Now when they heard this, they were cut to the heart, and said to Peter and the rest of the apostles, "Men and brethren, what shall we do?" Then Peter said to them, "Repent, and let every one of you be baptized in the name of Jesus Christ for the remission of sins; and you shall receive the gift of the Holy Spirit* (Acts 2:37-38).

In the last book of the Bible, the Book of Revelation, the word *repent* occurs 12 times. It is no coincidence that the New Testament church began with repentance and the New Testament ends with using the word *repentance* 12 times. In the Book of Revelation, Jesus challenges the churches to repent and clearly declares the consequences of a lack of repentance. (See Revelation 2:5,16,21-22; 3:3,19; 9:20-21; 16:9,11.)

Repentance is not something we do only to be saved; it must become part of every Christian's lifestyle. Every time we see that we have erred and are heading the wrong direction, we must not quiet our consciences by being sorry, but repent from our hearts.

Things have not changed since the time Adam and Eve sinned in the Garden of Eden. If we are wounded and hurt, the people who have wounded us will be responsible for what they have done. It must not be our concern to judge them; we need to leave that up to God. Our concern needs to be how we respond. If our response is unforgiveness and bitterness, we need to repent. Instead of seeing ourselves only as victims, we need to see our own trespasses and turn from them.

We should not continue to live with deep wounds in our souls; we need to begin the journey on the road to healing, which begins with the first step—repentance. Many have tried to receive emotional healing, but have not taken the right steps in the right order. They may have asked God several times to heal them, have gone forward for prayer to many altars. Perhaps people laid hands on them in order for them to receive emotional healing. All these things are good, but we need to take the first step first. Remember, if we are not willing to take the right steps in the right order, we will never run the marathon.

ENDNOTES

1. *Strongs Greek Lexicon*, 3809.

2. *Online Bible Greek Lexicon* (Ontario, Canada: Timnathsera), 1651/

Reality Check

Do I truly understand repentance; how would I explain
it to others in my own words?

_____

_____

_____

_____

_____

_____

_____

_____

Has the Lord convicted me of any sins I need to repent of?
If so, what are they, and what am I doing about them?

When have I been sorry for my sins but did not truly repent?

Does my life show fruit of repentance? If so, which fruit?

What resentment toward the Lord do I need to repent of?

Where have I been engaged in blame shifting, and what am I doing about it?

Prayer

Dear God, I come to You for help. I need You to walk with me on this path to wholeness. Help me to see my part. Open my eyes to see where I need to repent. My pride so often gets in the way. So often I want to blame others for the state I am in. Help me to see where I held on to unforgiveness and bitterness. I humble myself before You and am willing to change my mind. I turn from my unforgiveness and bitterness. I release to You all grudges that I hold against others. I trust Your grace to help me continue in the right direction. I will not go back again to my old ways. Amen.

CHAPTER 6

Step 2—Forgiveness

Forgiveness is a choice, but healing is a process. To begin the process of healing, we must first forgive all those who wounded us. Forgiving others is a neglected subject in today's church. There is much teaching on the grace and mercy of God and the free forgiveness we can access through the sacrifice and death of Jesus Christ. These are important teachings, since they are the basis and foundation of our faith. I am grateful for men like Martin Luther who paid a high price to restore the great truth that salvation is a gift from God to us.

The subject of freely forgiving all those who wounded us has been widely neglected. If we want to receive healing for our wounds, we must first forgive all those who hurt us and sinned against us.

Let us look at the importance of offering forgiveness to those who wounded us. Jesus used strong words when He was talking about forgiving others. We all have to continually walk through the process of forgiveness.

When the wounds go deep, trust has been violated and life doesn't seem worth living anymore. The last thing we feel like doing is forgiving those who wounded us. Having been there myself, I understand what a struggle it can be to forgive others. If we learn to be obedient to our Lord and live a lifestyle of forgiveness, we will find true freedom and inner peace.

The Scripture makes no indication that it is an easy thing to forgive. Forgiveness is a form of death, because we die to our old nature and its desire to hold on to resentment and take revenge.

If we make the choice to forgive, we can rely on Jesus who lives within us to give us the ability to obey Him and walk it out. The apostle Paul understood this when he said the life he lives in the flesh, he lives in faith, faith in the Son of God that loved him and died for him (see Gal. 2:20). We need to learn to trust the Lord every step of the way in our lives here on earth. It is my prayer that through these pages, the Lord will enable many to take the next step on the road to freedom and wholeness.

Why Do We Need to Forgive?

The question why we need to forgive those who wounded us is a very legitimate one. It is a good thing to understand why we do the things we do. The Lord is more than willing to show us why we need to do the things *He* asks us to do, if we come to Him with an open heart.

In this chapter, a number of reasons are discussed about why we need to forgive. The primary reason, of course, is that it is a clear command of Scripture. But other reasons are also discussed about why forgiving others is not an option for anyone who wants to live a life of victory. These reasons help explain why it is so vital to forgive.

Reason 1—We need to forgive so that satan cannot take advantage of us.

As discussed in an earlier chapter, satan is the enemy of our souls. If we are fighting against an enemy, the last thing we should do is give the enemy a head start. If *anyone* has a head start, we need to make sure it is us.

The Scripture admonishes us to forgive so not to give satan an advantage over us. In fact, the apostle Paul tells us that we are not unaware of satan's plans. It is clearly his plan to destroy our lives and if unable to do so, to at least stop us from reaching our potential in God. If he cannot stop us through different attacks and lies, he will certainly try to get an advantage over us by keeping us from forgiving others.

> *...For if indeed I have forgiven anything, I have forgiven that one for your sakes in the presence of Christ, lest Satan should take advantage of us; for we are not ignorant of his devices* (2 Corinthians 2:10-11).

The apostle Paul tells the church in Corinth that he is putting them to the test, to see whether they are obedient or not. In what way does he want them to be obedient? He wants them to affirm their love and forgive the man who has sinned. How can the devil take advantage of us if we do not forgive those who sinned against us? Let's look at the different ways the enemy can gain an advantage over us through our unwillingness to forgive.

Reason 2—We need to forgive, so that we don't pray against ourselves.

Pray against ourselves? How ridiculous would that be? We pray *for* ourselves, but not against ourselves! When I went to elementary school in Austria, we had to stand up every morning and pray the Lord's prayer. Austria is a country with a strong Catholic background, but primarily unchurched. Thousands of people pray the Lord's prayer regularly, simply because they learned to do so from early childhood on. Most people have prayed the Lord's prayer one time or another.

In Matthew 6:12, Jesus taught us that we should ask our Father in Heaven to forgive us *as we forgive* our debtors. One day when I prayed this prayer in school, I felt convicted. I realized that every day I was asking God to forgive me in the same way I forgive others.

I saw that if I was unwilling to forgive others, I was actually asking God not to forgive me, since I asked Him that He would forgive me *"in the same way"* I forgive those who wounded me. If I would forgive half-heartedly I was asking God to forgive me half-heartedly too. My own need of God's forgiveness was clear to me; therefore, I understood that the only option I had was to forgive others too. Since we do not want to pray against ourselves, the Scripture leaves us no other choice but to forgive others too.

Reason 3—We need to forgive because of the unchanging law of sowing and reaping.

There are certain laws written into the universe that will not change, whether we believe in them or not. We can jump off a very high building, confessing and declaring from the time we jump until the time we hit the ground that we do not believe in the law of gravity, but it will not alter the fact that we will break upon the very law we chose not to believe in. The law will neither weaken nor alter through our unbelief. It will stand firm, because it is how God has made it to be.

When Jesus finished teaching the disciples how to pray in Matthew 6, He carried right on telling them about the law of sowing and reaping. He told them plainly that if they would not forgive others, neither would their Father in Heaven forgive them. In other words, they would reap exactly what they would sow. (See Matthew 6:14-15.)

The apostle Paul also tells us unmistakably that we will reap whatever we sow. (See Galatians 6:7-10.) He uses strong language, by telling us that if we live as if the law of sowing and reaping does not exist we are deceived and mocking God. The Greek word which is used in Galatians for *mocking* means to turn up ones nose or to sneer at.[1] Why should any sincere Christian choose to live in deception or mock God? Yet have we not all at times done just that? I certainly have. We may break this law of sowing or reaping because we do not understand it or are unaware of it; therefore, it is important to read and study the Scriptures and allow the Holy Spirit to teach our hearts.

We must be aware that it is deceptive to believe that because we have a revelation of a truth we are already walking in it. There is a major difference between *knowing* the truth and *walking* in it (see Matt. 7:24-27). We can also be easily deceived by the fact that we might not see the harvest of our seeds immediately. But let us make no mistake the harvest will surely come, even though it may be delayed.

If we have repentant hearts, there is always enough grace. I am confident, that before Jesus returns, He will have a Bride pure and holy, without spot or wrinkle of unforgiveness and bitterness.

Reason 4—We need to forgive because of the unchanging principle of the kingdom of Heaven.

When Peter came to Jesus, he asked Him if he should forgive his brother as often as seven times. He was proud of himself for being willing to forgive so generously. According to one Bible commentator, the Jewish Rabbis of that day taught people to forgive their brother who sinned against them *three* times. Peter was willing to go much further and forgive up to *seven* times. How did

Jesus respond? Did He praise him for being so much better than the Rabbis? By no means, instead Jesus simply told him a parable about the kingdom of Heaven.

In Matthew 18:21-35 Jesus tells the disciples a parable to help them understand the importance of forgiving others. The parable goes like this: A king wanted to settle his account with his servants. One servant owed him a very large sum of money which he was unable to pay. He begged the king to be patient with him. The king had mercy on him and forgave him all of his debt. The servant then saw a fellow servant who owed him a comparatively small amount. When he was unable to pay, the servant had him thrown into prison. When the king heard of it he became angry and threw the unforgiving servant into prison. Jesus concluded His story with the sobering words: *"So My heavenly Father also will do to you if each of you, from his heart, does not forgive his brother his trespasses."*

If we want to live in the kingdom of Heaven and experience the authority thereof, we also must abide by the unchanging laws of this Kingdom. We must understand that the laws of this Kingdom will not change in order for them to fit our situation, culture, or time. We are the ones who need to change in order to adapt to the laws of His Kingdom.

The principles of this Kingdom are the same today as they were at the time Jesus told this parable; it is an eternal Kingdom ruled by an eternal King who does not change. (See Hebrews 13:8.)

Understanding Our Own Need of Forgiveness

It is our human nature to believe that what others do to us is worse than what we do to others. Many times have we excused the things we did, but when others did the very same thing, we were quick to judge. If we could only see the wickedness of our own hearts, and the many times our Father in Heaven had mercy on us, we would be more merciful to others. The laws of the

Kingdom are clear: if we have received forgiveness, and refuse to forgive others, we will have no excuses. God Himself will hand us over to the torturers.

Let us make no mistake, throughout all eternity we will be unable to pay for our sin. Our sin deserves death. Our only hope is God's eternal Kingdom, where we can receive forgiveness as a gift through the death of Jesus Christ. Having received it freely, we also must offer it freely to those who have sinned against us.

Reason 5—We need to forgive because unforgiveness will poison us and cause us harm.

When it comes to unforgiveness, it is dangerous to belittle its importance. Our wounded hearts want to deceive us into believing that it will not really affect us. In the same way that just one drop of food coloring in a glass of milk will change the color of the entire glass, so will unforgiveness affect our hearts. It will not just affect a very small part of our lives; it will influence our entire lives. It will affect our relationship with God, with others, and with ourselves. We will be unable to live in real peace with God, others, or ourselves if we allow the poison of unforgiveness to remain in our lives.

Handcuffed to the Ones Who Wounded Us

It is easy for us to make the false assumption that if we hold on to unforgiveness, we hurt or punish those who have wounded us. This assumption is as false as it is to believe that if we drink poison it will harm our enemy.

The illustration of handcuffs has been very helpful to me. If we refuse to forgive, we handcuff ourselves to the very people who wounded us. Many people whom I have counseled were shocked by this thought.

The last thing any sane person would want to do is handcuff themselves to the person who wounded them. It is our natural instinct to avoid danger, pain, and hurt, not to lock ourselves to it. If we do not release the ones who have wounded us through real heartfelt forgiveness, we will chain ourselves to them.

They might live far away, we might have no more contact with them, they might even be dead, but we are still handcuffed to these people if we have chosen not to forgive them. They torment us in our thoughts, emotions, and many times even our dreams. They are ever present, and no matter how far and how fast we run, we cannot outrun them because we have made the choice to handcuff ourselves to them. Forgiveness on our part will cut these handcuffs and set us free.

Mary Cut the Handcuffs

One beautiful sunny day I took my young boys to the lake to enjoy a day out. I had a rubber boat and decided to take it out on the lake. With us was Mary, a woman old enough to be my mother. We had known Mary for several years because she and her husband frequently visited our church during their vacation. We rowed out on the lake that beautiful summer day and chatted about many wonderful things the Lord had done. We talked about the subject of forgiveness. Mary's story left a deep impression on me.

She told me that when she was a child her stepfather periodically threatened to molest her sexually. She lived in constant terror of him. Even after she had become a Christian, was married and had children of her own, nightmares in which her stepfather molested her continued to torment her. No matter how much she prayed, she found no release from these nightmares.

One day she came to realize that she needed to forgive her stepfather from all of her heart. After she decided to do that, her nightmares stopped. The handcuffs were cut, and she was free.

Forgiving Ourselves

It is not only important to forgive others, but also to forgive ourselves. We have all sinned and failed in many ways, and the enemy will try to keep us in bondage with condemnation, guilt, and shame about our past failures. He might use legalistic people who live under the law and not by grace to bring condemnation to us.

If we do not learn to forgive ourselves and move on, we will, by our own fault, influence our future negatively. As long as we live with unforgiveness toward ourselves, we will not allow the Lord to change us in the areas where we have failed. Once we have repented, we must forgive ourselves, as the Lord has forgiven us. We are all sinners, but Christ is an amazing Savior.

Pride, the Root of Unforgiveness

We were coming to the end of our conference in Texas. We had several great meetings throughout the weekend when we preached on the topic of how to be overcomers in life. One of the messages was how to overcome unforgiveness and bitterness.

At the end of the service, a woman came to us asking for prayer. She struggled to forgive herself for the things she had done wrong. Mike, who ministered with me, told the woman that her inability to forgive herself is rooted in pride, which she needed to repent of. He explained to her that it is pride to believe that any sin we have committed is greater than the sacrifice of Jesus on the Cross. Jesus laid down His life so we can freely receive forgiveness from our sin. If the sin is not too big for *Him* to forgive us, than *we* must forgive ourselves too.

It does not matter how much and how often we have failed, the sacrifice our Lord brought through the Cross of Calvary is enough to cleanse us from all unrighteousness (see 1 John 1:9). He is the Lamb of God who carried away the sins of this world; therefore, to hold on to our own past failures and not forgive ourselves when God has already forgiven us, can only be the result of pride.

As we read the epistles of the apostle Paul, we can see repeatedly what an amazing revelation and understanding of the grace of God he had. He understood that we are unable to earn the forgiveness of sin. Before his encounter with the Lord, he was a Pharisee who tried to live his life strictly by the law. After his God encounter, he was so aware of his own sinfulness that he called himself the chief of sinners (see 1 Tim. 1:15).

He had harshly persecuted the church of Jesus Christ. But when the Lord laid hold of Paul and revealed the truth of the gospel to him, he rejected the belief that our good works will make up for our failures. He fully embraced the forgiveness of the Lord, left his past behind, and pressed on to the goal in Christ Jesus (see Phil. 3:1-14).

Debi's Amazing Miracle

It was 1983; I lived in a small town in the south of England. I was in my final year of Bible school, and I was getting ready to graduate. Debi and I were engaged, knowing that the Lord had called us to serve the purposes of His Kingdom together. Our backgrounds and upbringings were very different. We were opposite in most things, but one thing we had in common—we wanted to serve the Lord, please Him, and be obedient to Him in everything.

As we grew in our relationship and talked more openly about many things, we also talked about our pasts. Her dad left the family when she was young, and her mom did the best she could to raise her two kids. At the age of 18, Debi left home to join the Air Force. In her search for love and acceptance she got into relationships where men used her sexually, and at the age of 20 she had an abortion.

One day the Lord promised Debi that He would restore her virginity. Since the Lord had truly forgiven her past sexual sins, surely He was also able to do this miracle.

On October 25, 1986, Debi and I got married in the city of Graz in Austria.

After the wedding reception, we drove west and stayed in the suite of a beautiful Austrian hotel. This was the night Debi lost her virginity. God performed a miracle and restored her virginity. This is how much the Lord loves and forgives us. He did not just forgive Debi of all her sexual sins, but he also saw the desire of her heart and physically restored her virginity. It was one of the most awesome and sacred moments of our married life.

Defeating the Accusations of the Enemy

Since the Lord forgives us completely and does not hold our sin against us, as discussed previously, we also must forgive ourselves completely. We must shake off the lies of the enemy of our souls and release ourselves from the guilt and shame of our failures. Christ has paid for our sins once and for all, and that is enough. We must turn our wounds into scars and trophies of His grace!

Rick Watkins, a dear friend of mine who is a missionary in Poland, shared how he deals with the accusing voice of the enemy. When he sins and the enemy throws accusations against him, he does not argue with the enemy trying to belittle his failure. He simply tells the enemy that his accusations are true. However, the sacrifice of Jesus Christ is so complete and enough to pay for all of his sins. He has confessed and received forgiveness; therefore, none of the accusations of the enemy is valid—the blood of Jesus dealt with them all. Rick praises the Lord for His mercies and His magnificent heart that forgives even the vilest sin. He declares how wonderful is the God who removes our sin from us as far as the east is from the west. And his experience is that when the enemy's accusations are used as a stepping stone for praising God, the accusations are rendered powerless and soon cease.

Walking in Love

The Scripture tells us that even if we walk in the anointing and power of God, have enough faith to move mountains, and have outstanding revelations, but if we have no love, we are nothing. The Amplified Bible even says that we are useless nobodies.

> *And if I have prophetic powers (the gift of interpreting the divine will and purpose), and understand all the secret truths and mysteries and possess all knowledge, and if I have [sufficient] faith so that I can remove mountains, but have not love (God's love in me) I am nothing (a useless nobody)* (1 Corinthians 13:2 AMP).

Whatever we do must be motivated by love. To love the Lord our God and our neighbors as ourselves is the highest commandment.

If we truly love people and understand how destructive unforgiveness is, we will inevitably make an effort to help them to forgive. There might be people who are offended at us for no reason; still love will seek a way to help these people come to release through forgiving.

Answered Prayer for Eddy

I work at a school and it is part of my job to stand in the car line every morning and direct the traffic as the parents drop off their children. The principal of the school explained to me the traffic rules and told me to enforce them. Some parents did not like these rules and continually tried to break them.

Eddy was one of these parents. One morning he pulled his car into the parking lot, walked toward me angrily, and told me his opinion. I remained friendly and simply informed him that these are the school rules set by the principal and I have to enforce them.

Every morning as I directed the traffic in the car line I greeted all the parents with a friendly smile and waved to them. Eddy looked angry and turned the other way as I greeted him. This went on for several days. Then I decided to pray for him every morning. I interceded that the Lord would bless him, do him good, give him the grace to let go of his offense toward me, and forgive me. I prayed faithfully for many weeks.

I clearly remember the morning his car came around the corner again. This time instead of looking angrily the other way, he smiled back at me and waved. I praised the Lord for his faithfulness and his answer to my prayer. From that day on, he greeted me friendly every morning.

ENDNOTE

1. *Online Bible Greek Lexicon*, 3456.

Reality Check

When have I been praying against myself by not forgiving others?

_____

_____

_____

_____

_____

_____

_____

How does it make me feel when I ask the Lord to forgive me the same way I forgive those who wounded me?

Do I really believe that the Lord forgave me? When did I last thank Him for His wonderful forgiveness?

Do I still hold on to unforgiveness toward myself?

Which failures of the past do I still feel condemned about?

Who should I pray for in order for them to find grace to forgive?

Prayer

Father in Heaven, I thank You that You offer me your forgiveness with no strings attached. I am aware that without Your forgiveness I could not stand before You, because you are a holy God and I am a sinful human being. I understand that it is important for me to forgive all those who sinned against me. I also understand that I need to forgive myself and let go of any resentment I hold toward You. Help me to forgive just as You have forgiven me. Amen.

CHAPTER 7

Step 2 Continued—How to Forgive

There is much misunderstanding about the subject of forgiveness. There are numerous reasons for this. One of them is that the biblical meaning of forgiveness is often not understood. Another is that the enemy of our soul does not want us to forgive so he can hold us in bondage; he does not want us to enter our God-purposed destiny.

According to *Strong's* lexicon of the Greek, the word *forgive* is *aphiemi.* One of the meanings of this word is to send away. I found this word 146 times in the New Testament; it has a strong meaning. The same Greek word is used for divorce.

According to the law of Moses, under certain circumstances a man could write a certificate of divorce, give it to his wife, and send her away. (See Deuteronomy 24:1-4.) This is what it means to forgive. It means that we send away the sin that was committed against us. There is no more place for it in our lives. There are two Scriptures that use this Greek word.

*I came forth from the Father and have come into the world. Again, I **leave** the world and go to the Father* (John 16:28).

*They immediately **left** their nets and followed Him* (Matthew 4:20).

Here we can clearly see that the meaning of this word is a proper "leaving," as in going away. How many times have we forgiven with our minds and even with our words, but in our hearts we still hold on to the sin committed against us? This is not true forgiveness.

The Helpful Illustration

I once asked the Lord to help me better understand the true meaning of forgiveness. I wanted an illustration to help people forgive in a biblical way, in order for them to take the right steps toward healing and freedom. Since the time the Lord first gave me this beautiful picture, it has helped many people.

When I was a child, I loved helium balloons. When a new store opened in town or when there was some special celebration, people would hand out free helium balloons. Whenever I had the chance, I would do whatever it took to get one. To make sure the balloon got home safely, I held it tightly.

One day on the way home from such an event, I was careless and did not hold on to the string tightly enough. The helium balloon slipped out of my hand, and before I could do anything, it was gone. I stood there crying because my balloon went higher and higher with no way of retrieving it. I kept staring into the sky until I could see it no more. It was gone; there was no way I would get it back.

As the Lord brought this picture back into my mind, I realized that this is how we need to forgive. When I need to forgive and find it difficult, I go before the Lord in prayer. With closed eyes, I imagine holding a helium balloon in my hand. In my mind's eye, I take a marker and write down the name of the person I need to forgive. I might also write down the things done against me. Then I release the balloon and let it fly away. In my mind I watch it as it flies up into the sky farther and farther away. I then say to the Lord, "There it goes, it is flying up toward You. I release it to You. Now it is no longer mine but Yours. I refuse to hold on to it and gladly let it fly away."

Often our selfish nature is not willing to let go completely. We take the balloon inside our comfortable homes and then play the act of forgiveness half-heartedly. Now the balloon has only reached the ceiling and we are able to retrieve it anytime we want to.

You might want to verbalize your forgiveness in a way that is helpful to you. You might even go to the store and buy some helium balloons, write the names of the people you need to forgive on them, and literally let them fly into the sky. Whatever helps you to truly forgive, do it. Don't just do it in your heart, but be sure to confess it with your mouth.

A commonly asked question is whether all of the memories disappear with the act of forgiveness. I have met people who said that if we still remember the sins committed against us we have not truly forgiven. After all, the Scripture says that love covers a multitude of sin (see 1 Peter 4:8). I believe it is important to trust the Lord not only with the healing of our wounded hearts, but also with the healing of our memories.

The pain is often attached to the memory of the incident that wounded us. Therefore we need to ask Jesus to heal our memories. But Jesus can only help after we release the incident to Him. As long as we hold on to it through unforgiveness or resentment, we have not released it; therefore our pain will remain attached to us. Suppressing the pain or learning to live with it does not solve the problem.

Even though we have truly forgiven our offenders, the memories will remain stored in our soul. If unhealed, they will remain painful memories. But when Jesus heals our memories, they will become memories like the scars we talked about. They are not painful memories, but memories that remind us that the power of the Cross, which has enabled us to forgive and overcome the painful things done against us.

Our feelings will follow the decision once we truly forgive. There will be a period of time when we feel sore, but as we move forward in the healing process, these feelings will change too.

Let us remember that the meaning of forgiving is to let go and send away. We must write that certificate of divorce and send the sin committed against us away. There is no more room for it in our lives.

How Often Do We Need to Forgive?

As mentioned previously, when Peter asked Jesus how often he needed to forgive his brother who sinned against him, Jesus told him the parable of the unforgiving servant (see Matt. 18:21-35).

In this parable Peter was willing to go much further than the Rabbis and was hoping for the approval of Jesus for his spirituality, Jesus told him how often he needed to forgive—not seven times, but 70 *times* seven.

Some think Jesus meant that we should literally forgive 70 times seven, which is 490 times a day. When we take a closer look at the parable, we can see that Jesus even went a step further.

According to *Strong's* Greek dictionary, one meaning of the word *seventy* times is countless times. This interpretation seems more plausible, since the king who settled the accounts did not set a limit on his forgiveness. The debt of the servant was phenomenal; it was impossible to pay back under any normal circumstances. The king did not negotiate with the servant or offer installments; he simply forgave him and completely released the servant of all of his debt. Therefore our forgiveness cannot be limited. It is not a deed of the law, but rather a deed of compassion and love that will offer itself countless times with no limit.

When people have sinned against us, we may have forgiven their sin and let the balloon fly. The pain and the memory of it may still be present until the Lord has healed it completely. We need to understand that it is the nature of the enemy to keep accusing us of not having forgiven. The pain that is still in our soul might yell at us that we have not forgiven. Keep speaking out forgiveness, and keep those balloons flying. Not seven times, not 70 times seven, but countless times. Let's make up our minds that even if the whole sky has to be filled with balloons, we will always forgive and let go.

As Christ Forgave Us

Bearing with one another, and forgiving one another, if anyone has a complaint against another; even as Christ forgave you, so you also must do (Colossians 3:13).

The Scripture admonishes us to forgive in the same way Christ forgave us. Do we forgive others the same way that Christ has forgiven us? Or maybe we should ask the question differently. Would we want Christ to forgive us the exact same way we have forgiven others? Does it make us feel uncomfortable when we imagine that there is no difference between the way we have forgiven others and Christ has forgiven us?

Looking at the life of Stephen, the first-mentioned martyr in the New Testament church, and comparing it with the life of Christ, we can see that both men forgave the same way.

Then Jesus said, "Father, forgive them, for they do not know what they do..." (Luke 23:34).

And they stoned Stephen as he was calling on God and saying, "Lord Jesus, receive my spirit." Then he knelt down and cried out with a loud voice, "Lord, do not charge them with this sin." And when he had said this, he fell asleep (Acts 7:59-60).

I am thankful that when the devil stands before the throne of God to accuse us, Jesus does not stand there in agreement with him, but instead makes intercession for us. Such is the Spirit of Christ, and so complete is His forgiveness. In the same way and in the same spirit, we also must forgive those who sinned against us. (See Revelation 12:10 and Romans 8:34.)

The Process of Forgiving

Forgiving others is a process. The process does not have to take a long time, but we must walk through the process so that our forgiveness is sincere. We need to keep in step with the Lord and obey His Word.

Too often we rush to speak forgiveness only to find out that we have not really forgiven from our hearts, but just with our mouths. It could be that we wanted to ease our conscience, since we know in our heads that we need to forgive. However, God looks at our hearts. Let's walk through the process of forgiving.

Step 1—Calling things what they are.

We need to start by calling things what they are. We need to admit when others have sinned against us, or wounded us. It is secondary if the other person has actually wronged us or not. This is not really the issue when it comes to forgiving. If we perceive that someone wounded us, we need to release that person from what we believe he or she did against us.

It is for our own sake that we forgive. People have a threshold for pain, physically and emotionally. The intensity we can endure varies from person to person. Some people's temperament gives them a head start; some are born with a thicker skin. Therefore, it is important that we forgive when we feel that people wounded us whether others say they wounded us or not.

How many times have we made the following mistake: People do something that we perceive was wrong. In fact, we are sure that it was not right, especially if the person is a Christian. Then they come and tell us that they are sorry. Instead of dealing with the situation appropriately, we are quick to tell them that it is OK and there is no problem. But we have already complained to others or maybe even to the Lord about what these people did. It could be fear of others or our desire to be accepted that caused this reaction. However, it is unhealthy to deal with the problem in this way. We must accept their apology, speak forgiveness to them, and release them from their debt against us.

How can we begin the process of forgiving someone if we are not honest enough to admit that we were wronged? Our false politeness, which really is hypocrisy and dishonesty, causes us to marginalize things. Our fear of offending fools us, but the offenses against us are written on our hearts—if not dealt with, they will cause resentment.

As we grow in the Lord and in maturity, we learn to overlook many things and walk in love that covers a multitude of sins. We learn not to be wounded by those little scratches that happen as we walk on life's path.

Become aware of how sincere you are when accepting someone's apology. Be honest with yourself and the other person.

Step 2—Understanding our own sinfulness.

The king in the parable we discussed earlier was so angry against the servant he had forgiven, because the servant did not understand his own sinfulness. The debt he owed the king would be the equivalent of millions of dollars today. Make no mistake; the debt the fellow servant owed the other servant was also no small amount. He owed him one hundred denarii, the equivalent of one hundred day's wages. This is the same amount as if we were to work five days per week, which is 20 days per month, or equal to approximately five months' wages—a lot of money. The issue was not how large the amount was that the servant had to forgive his fellow servant, but how large the amount was that the king had forgiven him.

If we allow the Holy Spirit to show us our own sinfulness and the astonishing grace and mercy of our Father in Heaven, we will see things in a different light. Those who are forgiven much love much. Those who love much will in turn forgive much. It is important that we always remind ourselves about how much we have been forgiven.

Jesus tells us not to judge others. He calls people hypocrites who try to remove the splinter from their brother's eye without having their own plank removed first (see Matt. 7:1-5). As long as we live on this earth we will not be perfect; therefore, we need to leave it up to the Lord to be the Judge. He can see clearly, with no distorted vision.

Step 3—The surrender of self.

Jesus tells us that anyone who wants to be His true follower must take up his cross daily and deny himself (see Luke 9:23). This does not mean that we are to deny ourselves our God-given needs. God has created us with basic human needs such as food, water, shelter, a sense of belonging, etc. Denying means that we must not give in to the desires of our old sinful nature.

Our old sinful nature is unwilling to forgive others. To forgive is an experience of death. If we want to be true followers of Jesus Christ, we have to surrender our own sinful ways and desires.

The fear that we will lose our lives when we forgive is typical for our old nature, which wants to have full control of our lives.

However, Jesus clearly states that whoever wants to keep his life will lose it. (See Luke 9:24.) True life, which is the life of our risen Savior Jesus Christ, can only be found when we surrender our sinful desires to Him. When we understand that no one deserves forgiveness, we will offer this act of mercy freely to others.

Step 4—Letting go of self-defense.

Did you ever notice how quickly we defend ourselves when someone says something against us? The fear of losing our reputation can drive us to defend ourselves, even if what was said was accurate. Why is there such a desire to defend ourselves? There are various reasons. We might want others to think highly of us or desire their praise. Maybe we never had the chance to live in a safe and secure home where our parents protected us. Maybe we lived through abuse and the only way we could feel safe was to defend ourselves.

As followers of Christ, we must learn to live in complete trust in Him. The Bible is full of promises assuring us that God is on our side. The answer to every one of our problems can be found in the Lord. There is nothing He can't do.

How many times have we tried to defend ourselves only to find out that things would have been much better in the hands of the Lord? This has certainly been my experience. When Jesus went to the Cross, he could have easily defended Himself. In the garden of Gethsemane He let go of His self-defense and surrendered His life into the hands of his Father. (See Matthew 26:36-53.)

Jesus told Peter that it would be no small problem to get 12 legions of angels to defend Him. Before His arrest, He had already surrendered His desire for self-defense to His Father. He asked his Father in the garden of Gethsemane that if possible He should let this cup pass from Him, but that ultimately God's will should be done. Right then He surrendered His desire for self-defense. It took complete trust in his Father to do this, believing that God would raise Him again from the dead.

Is not our lack of trust that God will take care of us the reason we find it hard to let go of our desire for self-defense? Is it not pride to believe that we can defend ourselves better than the Lord can? How many times has the desire to defend ourselves caused us to hold on to unforgiveness and bitterness? If we truly want to forgive and let go, we must let go of the desire to defend ourselves and entrust our lives into the hands of our Lord.

Reality Check

Are there people whom I have forgiven from my head and with my mouth, but not from my heart?

Do I need to fill the sky with balloons? If so, what will be written on these balloons?

Am I truly aware of my own sinfulness?

Which areas of my life am I not willing to completely surrender to Jesus?

_____

_____

_____

_____

_____

_____

_____

_____

_____

Who do I harbor resentment against because of false politeness on my part?

Prayer

My dear Father in Heaven. I can see how freely You have forgiven me. I want to obey You and walk in total forgiveness. I am weak, but You are so strong. I ask You for the grace to forgive all those who have sinned against me and wounded me. I make the conscious choice to forgive and release all people against whom I hold unforgiveness. Holy Spirit, please bring to my mind all those whom I need to forgive, and walk me through the process of forgiving. Help me and direct me as I walk the path of forgiveness. I trust you completely. Amen.

CHAPTER 8

True Stories of Forgiveness

All the stories in this chapter are true. The people who experienced them wrote the stories themselves. I have known all of the people for many years and asked them to tell their stories in their own words. All the names have been changed, though, to protect their privacy.

Cassandra

Our family was cheated out of a large sum of money. It was the unrighteousness of the whole situation that made me angry. It was hard to forgive the person who swindled us. I wanted to forgive but was having problems due to the way the whole situation came about. I felt cheated and treated unfairly. I was used to forgiving people who had done me wrong because I usually played a role in the situation, meaning I was partly to blame for what they had done against me. But this person, who I felt acted maliciously against us for no apparent reason, I had to forgive over and over again but still felt no release from the whole thing. I was struggling terribly.

One day the following way of forgiving was explained to me: I was to envision a helium balloon. I should write that person's name on it and pray, forgiving that person for everything he had done to me, and then release the balloon to the Lord and in my mind's eye visualize it going up.

Well, I did it. The whole sky over the village was filled with helium balloons; I did get my release from my unforgiveness. I was truly over it and felt it in my heart.

Then the Lord did something that I thought was amazing. He not only gave me His peace again (which alone would have been more than enough), but He also blessed us with over three times the amount that was stolen from us. That was something I was truly not expecting, but I was thankful for it and His goodness.

Matt

Linda and I have been married for about seven years. I have been a Christian for about one year, Linda for about two years. Our daughter Sue is six and our son Mike is four years old.

It all started with a dream I had one night. In this dream I clearly saw that Linda had a sexual relationship with two men I did not know. Through certain details in the dream, I knew that this must have happened before we got married, but while we were already in a serious relationship. The dream was very real and vivid. Somehow I knew the dream was true.

I became very angry with Linda. While she was asleep next to me, I complained to God. "God, if this is true and if You are showing me this, I will wake her up immediately and confront her about it." I was angry and hurt, and in my mind I went over the things I was going to say to her.

However, God spoke to me: "First take the splinter out of your own eye." Immediately I realized that while I was already in the serious relationship with Linda, I also had a sexual relationship with another woman. At that time neither of us were Christians, and we never talked about the things that happened before we got married. After I got saved, I spoke to my pastor and told him about this event in my life, but I never told Linda. When Linda got saved, she wanted to confess her sexual sin to me but wanted to wait for a more opportune time, since I was not a Christian at the time.

As I lay on my bed and saw my own sin with my mind's eye, I felt true remorse about it for the first time. I was deeply shocked about what I had done. As the morning came and Linda woke up, I told her straight to her face what I saw in my dream. For a moment she was silent, and then she looked at me and said that she believed the dream was of God. She wanted to talk to me about it that evening.

It was a very long day. The whole day my mind was playing games with me. When the evening came we put our children to bed early and talked. As Linda told me her story, she was amazed about the details God had shown me in the dream.

Then it was my turn. I also confessed the affair I had at the beginning of our relationship. After we had confessed our sins to God and to one another, we decided to forgive each other. This was no easy thing; however, we felt an amazing release once we had truly forgiven one another. The rest of the evening together was very pleasant.

Soon after we went to bed our four-year-old son Mike came to our bedroom very excited. When we asked him what happened, he shouted: "The men are gone! Where did the men go to?" We had no idea what he was talking about. He then explained to us that for a long period of time he saw dark men in his bedroom. They came every evening. They never spoke a word, but were always present. Suddenly they disappeared and did not return. We immediately knew who the dark men were and that they would not return anymore. His nightmares were over! This experience showed me how important it is to forgive one another and that unforgiveness has spiritual consequences that we often do not know.

Mary

When my mother turned 39, she became pregnant with twins, my brother and me. She already had three children to look after, helped to run a farm, and took care of my grandmother. On top of that, my dad was an alcoholic. The whole situation was very over-whelming for her.

We grew up in a small Austrian village. My grandmother, who lived on the farm, lost her husband during the war, but she continued to run the farm with my mom and her younger son. Grandma gave her sister Vicky a piece of the land, on which Vicky built a house right across from us. Great Aunt Vicky's husband Ralph was always at home because he was unable to work from a war-related injury.

As a child I often wandered around daydreaming and totally lost, not knowing what to do with myself. My Great Uncle Ralph abused my search for love and began to take advantage of me sexually from a very early age. He abused me until the age of 12, when I was taken to a hospital to be treated for my psychological problems. Finally the whole truth came to the light. I had to begin therapy, which was so hard on my mom she barely survived it.

When I turned 17, I began my search for God but did not become a Christian until I turned 21. I was raised a strict Catholic, and the truth that salvation is a gift from God that Jesus paid for and that I can receive it without having to earn it touched me deeply. The knowledge that through the death of Jesus I could receive forgiveness brought great freedom to my life.

I decided to forgive everyone who had wounded me, including my Great Aunt Vicky and her husband Ralph. Ralph had already died, but to make sure that I had truly forgiven him, I spoke out my forgiveness over him. Great Aunt Vicky was full of hatred toward my mom and me. She would curse my mom publicly, and although she moved away from our village, she continued to speak words of hatred every time she saw us.

Even though I had forgiven her, I still lived in fear of her. One day I met her at the funeral of a neighbor and looked into her eyes and blessed her in my heart. Immediately I felt the fear of her leave me.

Later on I wrote her a letter and asked Aunt Vicky to forgive me. Because I wanted to help her be able to forgive, I decided to ask her to forgive me where I had hurt her. To my amazement, she wrote me a letter back and told me that I did need not to be afraid of her any longer. In her letter she reached out and forgave me. Today she is a very old woman. She is older than any of her siblings ever were and still rides her bicycle. She told other relatives that she has made peace with me.

Every time I think about it, I thank the Lord that He so freely forgave me, enabled me to forgive others, and used me to be a peace maker. I have decided before God to sign a blank check of forgiveness for all those who hurt me. This has made it so much easier to forgive people. It was not an easy task for me, but as I was willing and asked the Lord for his help, He worked in me and helped me to forgive.

Amanda (who is in her early 40s)

Since the spring of 2005, the Scripture, "you shall honor your father and mother" had been stirring my heart. I wrestled and argued with God, telling him that after everything my parents had done to me, I was unable to honor them. As long as I can remember, my relationship with my parents was superficial and distant.

From time to time I phoned them, and to fulfill my duty, I occasionally visited them. It hurt me that they did not really know me, or care about my feelings, thoughts, or me.

In July 2005 I phoned my parents and heard nothing but accusations about how little I cared about them. After our conversation, I burst out into tears, felt despair, and was full of anger and bitterness. The next day at a prayer meeting I burst out into tears again. Two women offered to pray for me, and when I told them my story, they encouraged me to forgive my father. In my head, I decided to forgive, but my emotions disagreed.

By the time the weekend came, the pressure to do something was so strong that I decided to visit my parents, who lived about 110 miles away. The entire trip, I listened to worship music, kept sobbing, and felt so wounded. During that time, two of my friends had offered to pray for me.

When I entered my parents' home, I felt a cold wall of rejection from my father. Crying, I asked if we could talk. He refused to talk to me, which brought all my suppressed emotions to the surface. I told him that I accepted him as a father, but could not accept the way he treated me. I told him that he never was there to protect me when I was suffering from sexual abuse as a child.

At this point he got up from his chair and began to laugh at me. He told me that all this was just in my imagination. I felt completely humiliated. By now I felt even more despair and sobbed uncontrollably. My mother came to my father's defense and told me that I could have gone to a psychiatrist if I needed help. Throughout the whole night, I laid awake on my bed and cried. Everything seemed so dark and hopeless.

In the morning, I went up on a mountain by myself and cried out to God for help. Where was God now, when I needed him? I happened to have the book *When God Writes Your Love Story* in my backpack. Aimlessly I opened the book and my eyes fell on a page where it talked about our relationship with our parents and the importance of forgiving them.

Suddenly I felt impressed on my heart that I needed to ask my parents to forgive me, where I, as their daughter, had disappointed them. I told God that that was too much for me to handle—I was unable to do that. Then God spoke to me and told me that with His help and support I would be able to do it, because He was with me.

After a lengthy discussion with the Lord, I decided to obey. I went back home and asked my father to forgive me. That very moment a miracle took place. Suddenly my father put his arm around my shoulder and told me that I had been a good daughter and that he was so sorry for everything that I had gone through.

Since then, my relationship with my parents has changed dramatically. My father cares about me and is even concerned about small details that matter to me. I want to encourage others through my story not to dwell in their wounded state, but rather to move forward and forgive. Forgiveness is a decision, but the healing of our emotions is a process.

Reality Check

Am I willing and humble enough to learn from others?

_____

_____

_____

_____

_____

_____

_____

_____

_____

Is there anything I still hold against my parents? If so, what do I hold against them and why?

When has the Holy Spirit nudged me to forgive and I have not obeyed?

Whom does the Lord want me to ask for forgiveness,
even though I feel that I am the abused one?

_____

_____

_____

_____

_____

_____

_____

_____

_____

Prayer

Lord, I thank You for others who have walked the path of forgiveness before me in order for me to learn from them. I can see the freedom others received through forgiving those who wounded them. Please help me to do the same, so that I can also be an example and an inspiration to others and lead them to freedom in Christ.

CHAPTER 9

Step 3—Asking Forgiveness

The obvious question comes to mind. "Why are we the ones who need to ask forgiveness when we are talking about how to find healing for the wounds others have caused us?"

This is not a discussion about whether we should ask those who have wounded us for forgiveness. At times this can be useful in order to release the grace of God to the ones who have wounded us, so they can ask us for forgiveness and make peace with us. Love will seek a way for others to be released from their unforgiveness.

In the light of what we have so far considered, we need to ask God for forgiveness. It is important that we understand what we need to ask forgiveness for and why; therefore, that is this chapter's discussion.

1. Asking forgiveness for our unforgiveness toward others.

As already seen earlier, to repent means to change our minds and turn around, which is an important part in the process. Nevertheless, repentance only gets us heading in the right direction, but it does not deal with the sin we have committed against the Lord and others.

We need to receive forgiveness from holding on to our sin of unforgiveness and bitterness. We have sinned against God by disobeying His command to forgive others, which He clearly shows us in His Word. Disobedience is a serious sin, which we must confess to the Lord and receive forgiveness for as we confess it. (See First Samuel 15:22-23.)

When King Saul disobeyed God because of his fear of men, the prophet Samuel made it clear to him; to disobey God is more than just a bad thing to do. He called rebellion against God's Word witchcraft. If we have disobeyed God by not forgiving, it is not enough for us to repent from our unforgiveness; we also need to seek and receive the forgiveness of God.

In order to receive forgiveness from the Lord, we need to follow some simple steps outlined in the first Epistle of John.

A. Admitting our sin.

If we say that we have no sin, we deceive ourselves, and the truth is not in us (1 John 1:8).

Take note that John is not writing to people who are not Christians, but to Christians who have already received Jesus as the sacrifice for their sins.

If we have come to realize that we still live with unhealed wounds and can only find release once we forgive those who have wounded us, we must also realize that the very unforgiveness we harbored against others is a sin and needs the forgiveness of the Lord.

When we are deeply wounded, it is easy to see the sin others committed against us and be blinded to our own sin of unforgiveness. The Lord is always willing to show us our own hearts, if we are willing to see them.

B. Confessing our sins.

There is a difference between admitting our sin and confessing our sin. Admitting our sin is to stop living in denial about it and realizing our sin of unforgiveness. We can do that without confessing it to the Lord as sin. We can admit our unforgiveness silently in our hearts, but in order to confess it, we must verbalize it.

The Lord can only forgive sin once we confess it as such. As long as we make excuses or try to call it mistakes, there is nothing to forgive. After all, mistakes are part of life and will happen to all of us. Sin is something we commit, and it must be confessed to the Lord as sin and nothing less.

C. Receiving forgiveness by faith.

John tells us in his epistle that if we confess our sin, God is faithful and righteous to forgive us our sin and cleanse us from all our unrighteousness (see 1 John 1:9).

We can only receive this cleansing by faith in the sacrifice of Jesus. No wallowing in self-pity or trying to pay for it will do. This only causes grief to the heart of God, since it is pride to believe that the sacrifice of Jesus is not enough and we are able to add something to it.

Remember what the word *forgiveness* means—to let go, to send away.[1] Once we have admitted and confessed our sin of unforgiveness, believed, and received forgiveness, it is gone. God does not hold on to it to bring it up should we fail again in the same area. No, it is gone; therefore, we also must let it go and forgive ourselves as He forgave us.

As far as the east is from the west, so far has He removed our transgressions from us (Psalm 103:12).

2. Asking forgiveness when our own sinfulness caused others to sin against us.

My ten-year-old son Danny was in fourth grade and getting ready to change schools. It was the end of the school year, and the teacher had planned a last field trip for the class. She invited the parents to join them on the trip.

As we hiked through the beautiful Austrian mountain, other kids started to tease a girl from Danny's class. Suddenly I found myself involved, because she was being teased because she was "in love" with my ten-year-old son. It seemed harmless and fun, and the girl did not seem to mind. I was unaware of my son's feelings and embarrassment.

As I hiked along beside these kids, I joined in the fun, which provoked Danny to anger. Suddenly I felt his teeth in my arm, biting me so strongly that it caused me to bleed, leaving marks, which were still visible days later. As I cried ouch, others around us were aware of what had just happened. I was upset at my son's reaction, or as I thought, overreaction, and scolded him.

Several days later, the Lord brought this incident back to my mind. Trying to process it and wondering whether I overreacted in scolding Danny, the following Scripture went through my mind.

And you, fathers, do not provoke your children to wrath, but bring them up in the training and admonition of the Lord (Ephesians 6:4).

Suddenly I became aware of my own sin, which provoked my son to become so angry that he wounded me. I talked to him about it, told him that I was sorry for what I did, and asked his forgiveness, which he gave me.

Whenever we process the sin others have committed against us, it is good to ask the Lord to show us if our sinfulness has in any way caused them to sin against us. Even though I was hurt, I had sinned against my son, but I also sinned against the Lord, since I disobeyed His Word in Ephesians 6:4. I asked the Lord and my son to forgive me for my sin.

We need to make this step part of our lifestyle. Every time others wound us and sin against us, we need to ask the Lord to show us if there is sin in our lives that has caused others to sin against us. If there is, we must not belittle it, but rather repent and ask forgiveness from the Lord and others to continue on our road to emotional healing.

ENDNOTE

1. *Online Bible Greek Lexicon*, 863.

Reality Check

When have I asked the Lord to forgive me for my unforgiveness toward others?

When and why have I given control of my life to someone else?

Am I aware of any sin in my life that causes others to sin against me? If so, what will I do about it?

Who do I need to ask for forgiveness when he or she sinned against me because of my own sinfulness in the event?

Prayer

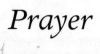

My dear heavenly Father, thank You for taking me a step further in the process of overcoming unforgiveness and bitterness. Let your Holy Spirit search my heart so I can see where I need forgiveness for my own sin. Show me things the way You see them. I am willing to confess my sin and receive your forgiveness. Amen.

CHAPTER 10

Step 4—Bless Your Enemies

Seal the Decision to Forgive

Jesus used some strong words in Matthew 5:43-45. He did not just tell us that we need to forgive and let go, He told us to go a step further. Jesus said:

> *"You have heard that it was said, 'You shall love your neighbor and hate your enemy.' But I say to you, love your enemies, bless those who curse you, do good to those who hate you, and pray for those who spitefully use you and persecute you, that you may be sons of your Father in heaven; for He makes His sun rise on the evil and on the good, and sends rain on the just and on the unjust."*

How many times have we forgiven people, but the offenses people have committed against us are still written on our hearts? How many times have we struggled, knowing that we need to forgive, but have gone ahead and forgiven people who wounded us? This is good and vital, but we need to take potential weapons out of the enemy's hand. The accuser of the brethren, the devil, will continue to accuse us of not having forgiven if any doubt remains in us. These accusations can be confusing, since we have already spoken out forgiveness to those who wounded us.

We must go a step further and seal our decision to forgive, which will defeat the accusations of the enemy. Jesus did not just tell us to love our enemies, but also to put actions to our love for them. Love without actions has no value. We must show through our actions that we love our enemies.

I am aware that at times this may be difficult. We may need to escape an abusive situation and set clear boundaries, while at the same time praying for those who hurt us. We will be able to do this with God's help, whether we are around those people or not. Once we begin to pray for the well-being of the people who used, wounded, and abused us, we will find that the accusations of the enemy will decrease and eventually cease.

I have made it a habit to counteract the feelings and accusations that I have not really forgiven by praying God's blessing upon the people who hurt me. What can the enemy say to a praying saint who intercedes for the people who wounded him? If we pray for and bless the people who hurt us, the accusations that we have not forgiven will cease. Our very actions prove that we have indeed forgiven. The Lord doesn't ask us to pray and bless our enemies when we feel like it; He simply tells us to do it.

Several years ago the Scripture about loving my enemies stirred my heart. I saw the heart of God, but was equally aware of my own weaknesses and inability to live this way. Therefore I decided to make it a matter of prayer. For weeks I prayed and asked the Lord to make me a person who is truly able to love my enemies.

At times it was difficult enough to love ordinary people who got on my nerves, never mind my enemies. But I was determined to follow the stirring of the Holy Spirit and kept asking the Lord to teach me His ways.

Then the Lord answered my prayer in a way I did not expect. Suddenly people close to me began to treat me differently. They would say and do things that hurt me, without being aware of what was happening. I tried to sort things out and talk to them, but with no results, since they were unaware of anything being wrong.

I took the matter to the Lord and asked Him what was going on and why there was suddenly so much strain on these relationships. The Lord reminded me of my prayer and asked me how I expected to learn to love my enemies if everyone was always nice to me. Thankful to the Lord, I began to practice and rejoice in the wonderful opportunities the Lord had given me. Not only did I change but, the people who hurt me soon changed to their actions too.

Being Overcomers

We need to learn to trust the Lord in all circumstances. He knows best how to take care of the things we need. It is normal for anger to rise up in us when we are wounded. The more we learn to trust God, the more we will believe that He is well-able to take care of our lives. As we learn to leave things in the hands of the Lord, we can learn to be true overcomers.

Scripture tells us that if it is possible we must live in peace with all people.

If it is possible, as much as depends on you, live peaceably with all men (Romans 12:18).

At times it will be difficult to do this because the other party refuses to be reconciled, but we must not feel condemned by this. This does not excuse us from blessing these people. If we seek His will, the Lord will direct us and show us ways to do this. He will let us know in what practical way we can bless those who wounded us and refuse to live in peace with us.

In Romans, the apostle Paul tells us that we should not be overcome by evil, but overcome evil with good. (See Romans 12:21.) We will have to make the choice whether we want to be overcome or be overcomers. Do we want to be dictated to by our circumstances, or do we want to dictate our circumstances? If we do not make the clear and conscious choice to overcome evil with good, we will be overcome by evil.

The Law of Sowing and Reaping

Therefore, whatever you want men to do to you, do also to them… (Matthew 7:12).

For judgment is without mercy to the one who has shown no mercy. Mercy triumphs over judgment (James 2:13).

As discussed earlier, this law is written as firmly into the universe as all the other laws God established. Reminding myself of this Scripture in Matthew 7 where Jesus asks us to do to others what we want them to do to us has been very helpful whenever I need to forgive and pray for those who wound me. What is it that I would like others to do to me when I have failed and hurt them, or even sinned against them? Do I want people to gossip about me, pray against me, curse me, or do I want them to forgive and bless me?

Since Jesus told us to do unto others whatever we want men to do unto us, I keep reminding myself that I want others to bless me. Therefore I make the choice to do the same. As discussed earlier, we will always reap what we sow. There might be a long time between the time we sow the seed and reap our harvest, but let us not be fooled—the harvest will surely come and usually in a much greater abundance than the seed we planted.

How wonderful it could be if the Body of Christ would begin to sow blessings instead of cursing. What a great release of blessings and miracles it would bring. If we would turn every criticism into intercession, the Body of Christ would move forward as one mighty army. We do not need to be condemned when we have failed in this area. Repentance will change things and release the grace of God. Once a sinful deed is repented of, we can ask the Lord to destroy our harmful seeds. We can then begin sowing good seeds of blessings.

Reality Check

Which people have I forgiven and now need to pray for their blessing?

_____

_____

_____

_____

_____

_____

_____

In which practical ways can I bless those who wounded me?

To which people who wounded me do I need to extend mercy in order for me to receive mercy?

Is there a harvest of foul and bitter fruit in my life, and do I need to repent from sowing bad seed? If so, what is the seed I have sown?

Prayer

Dear God, I acknowledge that Your Word asks me to do things that are contrary to my old nature. However, I am a new creation in Christ Jesus, and I thank You for enabling me to act according to this new nature. Please show me where I have cursed people who have hurt me through my negative words, and even prayers, instead of blessing them. I will repent and begin to bless them and pray for them. Amen.

Chapter 11

Receive Healing

It is a common mistake to believe that because we have forgiven and even blessed the ones who hurt us that we are immediately free and healed. We must not stop at the place where we have forgiven, but rather we must realize that this is only the beginning.

We must move forward to receive healing for our wounds. Forgiving others and blessing them does not heal our wounded hearts—it releases the peace of God and brings freedom to us, but then the healing process must begin.

Many times we forgive those who wounded us, but the pain is still attached to that event. We might be confused and may not know what to do with the pain. We must seek healing for our wounds and memories. It is wonderful and amazing to see how God created us with the ability to feel pain. Pain shows us that something has gone wrong and we need to get to the root of the problem, solve it, and receive healing from it.

It is vital that we do not ignore our wounds and press on in life as if nothing ever happened. How we react and deal with our emotional wounds will, among other things, depend on our temperament, understanding, and upbringing. Our temperament and understanding will largely determine how we react and deal with our emotional wounds. If we do not fully understand how important it is for us to be emotionally healed, we are in danger of pushing through the pain and living our lives as if nothing ever happened to us. But wounds need to be healed, because *hurt people hurt people, and healed people heal people.*

I have heard bestselling author Rick Joyner say on several occasions, "There is a ditch on either side of the path of life." As dangerous as it is to ignore our woundedness and keep going, it is equally dangerous to sit in self-pity and cry about it. Wounds need to be healed, not licked. Being aware of our woundedness and crying about it will not bring us to healing. We need to face our wounds, walk through the right steps, and come to the only Source for healing, the Lord, Jesus Christ.

Remember, forgiveness is a choice; healing is a process. We are very complex beings, not simply programmed computers. The Lord will bring healing to us in many different ways. The Lord uses different ways to heal our emotions, just like He uses different ways to heal our bodies. I have seen many physical healings through the hand of the Lord in many different ways, from instant, miraculous healings, to gradual healings. It is important that we never limit the Lord in the ways He will heal our wounded hearts.

Seeing Our Need

Sometimes it is easier to live in denial than to face the fact that there are emotional wounds that need healing. Men especially have the tendency to be tough and ignore their pain. Even if we learn to live with our emotional wounds, that is not the answer to solving the problem. There is no such thing as an unexpressed emotion. If we deny, suppress, or ignore our emotional wounds, they will find expression elsewhere—usually negatively.

It took me a good while and the gracious work of the Lord to come to the realization that I needed the Lord to heal my wounds. I did not like the thought that I, someone who likes to bungee jump and be adventurous, needed healing for my emotional wounds. My approach to this subject was simply to get over it and move on. The Lord in His mercy and grace, however, found a way to get me to surrender and allow Him to bring healing to my heart.

Jesus told the Pharisees that those who are well have no need of a physician. He was referring to the Pharisees who believed they were righteous, when in reality they were far from it. (See Mark 2:15-17.) Only when we recognize our need for our emotional healing can the Lord begin His wonderful healing process in us.

Jesus—the Only Source

While there are many *ways* to our healing, the only *Source* of our emotional healing is the Lord. No matter how much professional help we receive and how well we understand the reasons for why we feel the way we do, or why we act and react the way we do, true healing can only be found through the Cross of Jesus Christ.

The Lord may choose to use different channels to bring healing to us, but the source is the Lord. This will help us to rest confidently in him, since it does not matter which means or which channel the Lord decides to use to bring healing to us. Our confidence is not in the tools he uses, but rather in the Master who cares enough about us to bring us healing.

Every good gift and every perfect gift is from above, and comes down from the Father of lights, with whom there is no variation or shadow of turning (James 1:17).

James reminds us that the source of our good and perfect gifts is our Heavenly Father who has only pure motives toward us. Through Jesus, who went about healing all those who were oppressed by the devil, he revealed the heart of the Father to us (Acts 10:38).

It is vital that we do not seek healing from men, but rather from our Lord, who is the source of all good gifts. If we can truly repent from our pride, which so often hinders us from receiving through the channels the Lord decides to use and turn from our unbelief, we will find that the Lord will be able to bring healing to us.

This will also help us to relax, since we do not need to spend all our energy and resources running after the great healers. We simply need to trust the Lord that He will bring healing and then learn to listen and obey Him; He will lead us to the channels He decides to use for our healing.

Be assured that the Lord who loves us and created us, body, soul, and spirit, is touched with our pain and suffering. As the prophet Jeremiah said, when the Lord heals, we are healed indeed (Jer. 17:14).

Being open to the Lord

As mentioned earlier, there are many ways the Lord will use to bring healing to us. The instruments and ways He uses are truly manifold; the source, however, is the Lord and His work on the Cross.

In the Bible, we find many accounts of physical healing. The Lord healed people in many different ways. He healed them through speaking words of healing to them, casting out demons, giving them instructions to do something, allowing them to touch His clothes, and other ways. (See Matthew 8:13; 9:20-22 and Luke 13:11-13; 17:11-14.)

The apostles experienced the healing power of God in different ways too. Peter commanded the man at the beautiful gate to get up and walk; others received healing as his shadow touched them. People took the handkerchiefs of the apostle Paul and found healing and deliverance. (See Acts 3:2-8; 5:14-16; 19:10-11.)

As the Lord uses manifold ways to heal people physically, He also uses manifold ways to heal us emotionally. As we seek healing for our wounded hearts, we must be open to the Lord for Him to do His work in whatever way He decides. He may use a wise counselor, your family, your home group, a simple prayer, or any other way He chooses.

Reaching Out in Faith

Throughout the gospels we find people who needed a miracle from Jesus. Those people would reach out to Him, asking for their miracle. At times they even went out of their way and made great sacrifices to come to Jesus and receive healing. We need to come boldly before God's throne and ask Him to heal our wounded hearts. Jesus is more than willing to heal us, but *we* need to be willing to put our trust in Him by asking Him for our healing. (See Luke 4:18,20.)

He heals the brokenhearted and binds up their wounds (Psalm 147:3).

The Psalmist declares that the Lord not only heals the brokenhearted, but He also "binds up their wounds." This speaks of a loving and caring action. If our picture of the Lord is one of a hard taskmaster, we will not dare to come to Him with our wounds. When we are wounded, the last thing we want is to come to someone who treats us carelessly. The Lord is not just interested in healing our broken hearts, but also in binding up our wounds so that they can heal.

In Luke 4 when Jesus came into the synagogue, He opened the scroll to Isaiah 61. After He read the beautiful passage in which the Lord promises to heal the brokenhearted, Jesus told the people that these words were fulfilled right there and then.

The people marveled at the gracious words that came from His mouth. People were amazed because they were hearing from a tenderhearted man who was declaring that now was the time for the brokenhearted to be healed instead of the usual rules and regulations being declared in the synagogue.

Jesus has not changed, nor has His desire to be gracious toward the wounded in heart changed. We need to reach out in faith, believing that He is truly able to heal those wounds that are so deeply engrained in our hearts. He feels the pain we feel, and He desires for us to trust Him to be our healer. He is well-able to heal our wounded hearts and our memories if we only reach out to Him in faith.

Reality Check

What areas of my life need healing, and am I willing to let the Lord show me any areas I am still in denial about?

Have I made Jesus the only source of my healing?

Where do I run after others for my healing?

Am I open for the Lord to use any way He chooses to bring healing to my wounded heart? Which means of bringing healing do I reject?

In which ways am I reaching out in faith to the Lord?
Am I just waiting for things to happen?

Prayer

My heavenly Father, full of mercy and grace, I thank you for Your wisdom and kindness. I trust You for my healing and surrender myself completely to You. I hold nothing back. Do whatever You need to do to make me whole. Heal my wounded heart. Amen.

CHAPTER 12

Things the Lord Taught Me

Over the years God has taught me many wonderful and practical things regarding healing and wholeness. He used many wonderful people and resources, which He brought into my life at the right time. Time and time again, I have watched people ignore the following truths, only to find themselves isolated and even more hurt. The enemy will use hurt people to hurt people, while the Lord will use healed people to heal people.

Staying Connected to the Body

One great way the Lord uses to heal our wounded hearts is through the Body of Christ, which is the church. Even in the natural, the Lord has put it into the DNA of the physical body to heal itself. I am fully aware that in some cases the professional help of doctors is needed. But many injuries and hurts will heal naturally if we just rest and allow the body to heal itself.

In the same way, the Lord will use the Body of Christ to bring healing to us. We must not allow the enemy to cut us off from the Body and drive us into isolation just because we are wounded. Even though the Body might have wounded us, we must overcome our offenses and yield to the love and life of God, which will flow through His Body to bring healing to us. This is the way the Lord has designed it. If we wait until we find the perfect local church, we will be searching forever, because the moment we find and join it, it would no longer be perfect.

Several years ago, our family went through a very traumatic experience. We were rejected and wounded by parts of the Body of Christ, but we made a decision that we would not cut ourselves off from the Body. The Lord in His wisdom and grace has used different parts of the Body to heal the very wounds other parts of the Body caused.

As a boy, I used to daydream while walking through the streets of our small town. Many times I would be looking at everything except the sidewalk I was walking on. Consequently I would hit my head or scrape my knees because I would trip and fall.

My knees did not cut themselves off from the rest of my body because my eyes did not do what they were supposed to do. And it was not the fault of my knees that they were hurt; it was the fault of other body parts. My knees needed to heal, which they did as long as they remained part of my body.

Likewise when we, as part of the Body of Christ, are hurt, we must remain part of the Body so we can heal.

Yielding to the Process

Since healing is a process, we need to yield to the Lord for Him to do His work in us. Letting go of our unforgiveness and allowing the Lord to deal with all the poison of bitterness in our hearts is just the beginning of the healing process.

As a child I was very active and loved playing outdoors. Scraped knees and elbows were natural for me. Whenever these wounds would begin to heal and a scab would begin to show, I found it almost impossible to yield to the healing process. I would continually pick those scabs, which of course only caused me to bleed and slowed down the healing process.

In a similar way, we must not pick at our emotional scabs, but allow the Lord to finish the process He began in us. If we impatiently interfere every time the Lord begins a healing process in us, we only slow down the process. He knows what He is doing, and we need to learn to completely trust Him and surrender ourselves to Him for the healing of our wounded hearts. We must not underestimate the importance of yielding to the Lord.

When our son Danny was about four years old, my wife began to teach him how to tie his shoes. One day we had to go out, and I asked him to get his shoes and put them on. When I stooped to tie them, he assured me that he was able to do it himself. He refused to let me help him. I offered him my help several times, but he insisted that he was a big boy now and could do it.

As I stood and watched him struggle, I felt so helpless. I wanted to help him, but he refused to yield to Dad. Therefore, I stepped back and watched him getting more and more frustrated. After awhile, he yelled out, "Daddy, help me tie these stupid shoes. It doesn't work!" Gladly I helped him tie his shoes, which was only possible once he yielded to me.

As we learn to quit struggling in our own strength, and yield to the hands of Jesus, who is able and willing to heal our wounded hearts, we will experience the healing process.

Giving the Lord Time

I love the prophetic environment, and I am very thankful that the Lord allows me to be part of a great church that is very open to the prophetic and is used by the Lord to equip the Body of Christ in this area.

Not only do we need to understand what the Lord wants to do, but we must also learn to be in step with the timing of the Lord. When the Lord reveals His will and purpose to us, it is normal for us to get excited. We will be in great danger of becoming disillusioned and giving up if we do not understand the timing of the Lord. His Word will release faith in our hearts. But it is not by faith only that we inherit His promises, but by faith and patience (see Heb. 6:12). If we do not understand this important truth, we will give up instead of allowing the Lord to continue His healing process.

Jesus makes it clear in the parable of the sower that if we want to bring forth fruit it is not enough to receive the Word of God with joy. When tribulation comes and things do not go the way we want them to go, we might be tempted to give up. It is not enough to endure for just awhile; we must allow the Lord to do His work in our hearts in His time, not in ours (see Matt. 13:18-21).

We can have confidence that when the Lord begins a good work in us, He will also complete it. Therefore, time is not the issue, trust is. (See Phil. 1:3-6.)

Getting to the Root

The Lord longs to heal our wounds, but much more than that, He wants to get to the root of our problems. I am aware that we might be wounded simply because we live in a sinful world and being wounded is part of life; however, everything the Lord allows is for a reason. He will use even our very failures for His glory if we surrender to Him and are willing to learn every lesson He has for us.

If we always attract certain kinds of wounds, we need to ask the Lord to get to the root of our problem. We might live with inner vows, bitter root expectations, generational curses, or other spiritual dynamics with which the Lord needs to deal. It has been my constant prayer for many years that the Lord would not just deal with me superficially, but rather cleanse my heart thoroughly and take His axe to the rotten roots in my heart.

Since I've been continually praying this prayer for my family, I have seen the Lord answer in wonderful ways. No one knows how to better deal with bad roots in our lives than the Lord does, because He knows every hidden corner of our hearts. Make no mistake—a bad tree cannot produce good fruit. If we have rotten roots in our lives, we need to allow the Lord to deal with them, rather than just superficially pick the bad fruit off the tree, or just cover it up. It would be like removing the cobweb from time to time instead of getting rid of the spider.

Delivered From a Generational Curse

Our younger son Chris was very active from a young age on. He liked adventure and sports. When he got into sports, he did it wholeheartedly. For many years he suffered from frequent injuries like sprained joints, pulled muscles and ligaments, and the like. He was a regular patient in the emergency room. We attributed his frequent injuries to his temperament and his involvement in sports. However, the Lord began to show us that there was a deeper reason for the injuries.

My wife had mentioned to me several times that her uncle, whom she lived with for awhile, was a high-ranking Freemason. Since she never had anything to do with Freemasonry, I thought nothing of it. In October 2004, we obeyed the guidance of the Lord and moved from Austria to the United States. Shortly after our move, Chris joined the local soccer team. Sure enough, after only playing a few games, another player fouled him so badly that he was taken out of the game with an injured ankle. Chris ended up in the emergency room, was put on crutches for several days, and quit the team.

In the spring of 2005, my sister visited us for several days. She was in Kansas City for a three-month training program at International House of Prayer. During her visit with us, she shared with my wife Debi what she had learned about generational curses through Freemasonry and left her some reading material about it.

After my sister left, Debi asked me if we could spend some time together going through the material asking the Lord to reveal anything to us that He wanted us to know. Something caught our attention—frequent injuries in a relative of a Freemason can be part of a generational curse of Freemasonry. This revelation leapt off the page at us.

We brought it to the Lord, broke the curse, and trusted that the power of Jesus Christ would be sufficient. We did not tell our son Chris, since we felt no need to. The change was dramatic. Chris now plays on the high school soccer team, practices hard, and his frequent injuries have stopped. Now when he gets injured, it is because of the extreme way he plays and not because he attracts these injuries because of a curse.

It is not helpful to spend our time and energy constantly trying to dig for bad roots in our lives. We need to have confidence in the Lord who is our Healer and Deliverer to take care of us. If we allow Him to work in our hearts, long for Him to heal our wounded hearts, and surrender to Him, He will heal our wounds. If we are aware of bad fruit in our lives, we need to ask the Lord to show us the root so that we can allow Him to deal with it.

Praying for One Another

No man is an island. The Scripture compares the Church to a Body.

> *Now concerning spiritual gifts, brethren, I do not want you to be ignorant: You know that you were Gentiles, carried away to these dumb idols, however you were led.*

Therefore I make known to you that no one speaking by the Spirit of God calls Jesus accursed, and no one can say that Jesus is Lord except by the Holy Spirit.

There are diversities of gifts, but the same Spirit. There are differences of ministries, but the same Lord. And there are diversities of activities, but it is the same God who works all in all. But the manifestation of the Spirit is given to each one for the profit of all: for to one is given the word of wisdom through the Spirit, to another the word of knowledge through the same Spirit, to another faith by the same Spirit, to another gifts of healings by the same Spirit, to another the working of miracles, to another prophecy, to another discerning of spirits, to another different kinds of tongues, to another the interpretation of tongues. But one and the same Spirit works all these things, distributing to each one individually as He wills. For as the body is one and has many members, but all the members of that one body, being many, are one body, so also is Christ. For by one Spirit we were all baptized into one body—whether Jews or Greeks, whether slaves or free—and have all been made to drink into one Spirit. For in fact the body is not one member but many. If the foot should say, "Because I am not a hand, I am not of the body," is it therefore not of the body? And if the ear should say, "Because I am not an eye, I am not of the body," is it therefore not of the body? If the whole body were an eye, where would be the hearing? If the whole were hearing, where would be the smelling? But now God has set the members, each one of them, in the body just as He pleased. And if they were all one member, where would the body be?

But now indeed there are many members, yet one body. And the eye cannot say to the hand, "I have no need of you"; nor again the head to the feet, "I have no need of you." No, much rather, those members of the body which seem to be weaker are necessary. And those members of the body which we think to be less honorable, on these we bestow greater honor; and our unpresentable parts have greater modesty, but our presentable parts have no need. But God composed the body, having given greater honor to that part which lacks it, that there should be no schism in the body, but that the members should have the same care for one another. And if one member suffers, all the members suffer with it; or if one member is honored, all the members rejoice with it.

Now you are the body of Christ, and members individually. And God has appointed these in the church: first apostles, second prophets, third teachers, after that miracles, then gifts of healings, helps, administrations, varieties of tongues. Are all apostles? Are all prophets? Are all teachers? Are all workers of miracles? Do all have gifts of healings? Do all speak with tongues? Do all interpret? But earnestly desire the best gifts. And yet I show you a more excellent way (1 Corinthians 12).

We are in close connection to one another, and our lives will influence and affect each other. Often the people closest to us wound us, but we must also see that we have wounded people close to us. We must not allow this fact to take us into despair and depression, but rather use the very things the enemy meant for harm and turn them around for the glory of our King Jesus.

We all need to pray for one another. It is the heart of the Lord for everyone in spiritual authority to pray for the healing of the people entrusted to them. We can see this in the life of the apostle Paul how he constantly prayed for the people entrusted to him. We need to pray that the Lord will heal those with a wounded heart. Pastors need to pray for their churches, parents for their children, husbands for their wives, employers for their employees, and so on.

Taking Spoil From the Enemy

Jesus clearly predicted Peter's failure before Peter denied him. (See Luke 22:31-34.) Peter opened a door in his life to satan through his pride. As Jesus predicted his fall, Peter responded to the Lord by telling Him that he would not fail; he would even be willing to die for Him. It is noteworthy that Jesus did not pray that Peter would be spared from this failure; neither did he give Peter a lengthy lesson trying to save him from it. Jesus prayed for Peter that his faith would not fail. Jesus told Peter that God would use the very failure when He said, *"When you have returned to Me, strengthen your brethren!"* (Luke 22:32).

The goal and purpose was clear. The failure satan planned for destruction, God wanted to use for good. We also can use our very failures to the glory of our King, if we surrender to the Lord in repentance.

For a long time I grieved over the wounds I caused others, especially those who were close to me. One day I realized that the very pain I caused others, the Lord can use to bring glory to His name. I began to intercede for those I wounded knowingly or unknowingly. I prayed for healing of their wounds, for restoration, and for their faith not to fail. I prayed that the Lord would use these failures to further His purposes and extend His kingdom.

Remember that our scars are trophies. It is my prayer that God can use the wounds that I have caused others and turn them into their trophies of His grace. This is by no means an excuse to treat others carelessly or not to ask forgiveness when we are aware that we have wounded them. We need to learn from our failures and believe that the Lord can use even the things that have the potential to destroy other lives for His ultimate glory.

Reality Check

Have I cut myself off from the Body of Christ, and am I living in isolation?

How willing am I to yield myself completely to the Lord?

How much time am I willing to give the Lord to heal me?

How do I show my willingness for the Lord to go to the root(s) of my problem(s)? Whom have I wounded intentionally or unintentionally, and do I pray for them?

Prayer

Dear heavenly Father, full of mercy and grace, I thank You for Your wisdom and love. You know what is best for me. Help me to find my place in your Body of believers. Bless me and make me a blessing to others. Put the axe to every bad root in my life. Heal those I have wounded, and use the very wounds to glorify Your great name. I trust you. Amen.

CHAPTER 13

Keeping a Clean Heart

Keep your heart with all diligence, for out of it spring the issues of life (Proverbs 4:23).

The Scripture passage uses strong words to make us understand the importance of keeping our heart free from offense. The word used for *keep* in this verse is the Hebrew word *natsar* and was used to describe watchmen watching over the city. It does not mean to be relaxed, hoping that everything will be safe, but rather to be on active duty, as these watchmen were.

The word *diligence* is the Hebrew word *mishmar* and was used to describe prison guards who watched over the prisoners with diligence, making sure they did not escape. We are told to watch our hearts very carefully, since out of it flow the issues of life. If we neglect our hearts, the flow of life will be limited, unclean, or spoiled. How can we watch our hearts? Here are some ways:

1. Love the Lord With an Undivided Heart

Jesus made it clear that God does not want our superficial or half-hearted love. He wants us to love Him with all our heart.

*Jesus said to him, "'You shall love the Lord your God with **all** your heart, with **all** your soul, and with **all** your mind'* (Matthew 22:37).

Notice He did not say that we should love God just from our heart, but from *all* our heart. (See also Matthew 22:35-40.) It is all too easy to live with a divided heart, giving God only part of it. We must resist the many different things fighting for our heart's attention. One way of protecting our heart is to love God with all our heart and give Him the first place. We need to continually rededicate our hearts to the Lord.

2. Receive His Love

The questions arise: Can the Lord be satisfied with our human love? Will He be pleased with it? Is our love sufficient for the Creator of Heaven and earth? The answer to all three questions is no. The Lord wants us to learn to receive His love and be full of it so that our hearts will overflow with it. In turn, His love can flow out of us to the people around us and back to Him. We must constantly seek to understand, experience, and know more of the wonderful love the Lord has for us. This will drive out fear and insecurity from our hearts and enable us to keep our hearts clean. John states that we only love Him (the Lord), because He first loved us (see 1 John 4:19).

In the Song of Solomon, which illustrates the love between the Lord as the Bridegroom and the Church as the Bride, we see how much the Lord loves us. In Song of Solomon 4:9 the Bridegroom says to His Bride:

You have ravished my heart, my sister, my spouse; You
have ravished my heart with one look of your eyes....

It is hard for us to fathom the fact that the Lord would feel so
strongly about us, yet He does. We have captured His heart. His
heart is all for us, and His love is never ending. When we are hurt
and wounded, it is all too easy to project these pains onto the Lord.
Let me assure you that He loves you very much; you have truly
captured His heart. It must be a priority for us to continually grow
in His love for us.

I have developed a habit of staying in bed for a few moments
after I wake up, just quietly telling the Lord how much I love Him
and expressing my gratitude to Him. One morning after I woke up,
the Lord spoke clearly to my spirit. What He told me took me by
surprise. He asked me to begin the day with thanking and praising
Him for His great love for me and to enjoy soaking in it. When I
began this practice, it had an amazing outcome. After awhile my
heart was so overwhelmed with His love for me that it just flowed
over back to Him with expressions of love and thankfulness.

3. Enjoy the Feast

All the days of the afflicted are evil, but he who is of a
merry heart has a continual feast (Proverbs 15:15).

When our hearts are happy and cheerful, we will live in a continual feast. Feast speaks of abundance, joy, and celebration. The
Lord intended for us to live in His abundance. There is no lack in
Heaven, and since we are heading that way, we might as well begin
to practice feasting now. How can we live here on earth and enjoy a
continual feast? We must make the joy of the Lord our strength
(see Nehemiah 8:10). In His presence, there is an abundance of joy
(see Psalm 16:11). Worldly pleasure will last for a short while, but
the joy of being in His presence will be our strength even in times
of hardship.

4. Worship God

Speaking to one another in psalms and hymns and spiritual songs, singing and making melody in your heart to the Lord (Ephesians 5:19).

We need to learn to worship and praise the Lord in all circumstances. If we fill our hearts with praise and worship and express it toward the Lord, our hearts will be cheerful, which in turn will cause us to have a feast. I always enjoy the time when God's people meet and worship Him in unity. If we have not learned to worship Him in our private lives, how authentic is the worship we offer when we gather and the music is just perfect?

Don't be fooled; it does not depend on outward circumstances whether we are able to praise God from our hearts. The apostle Paul did not write Ephesians 5:19 as theory, but as something he practiced, even under severe circumstances (see Acts 16:16-25).

True worship is not what we bring the Lord when all things are perfect and our prayers are answered. If we want our hearts to be cheerful, we must learn the secret of worshiping the Lord in the privacy of our lives.

5. Keep a Humble Heart

We need to keep our hearts free from pride. There is plenty of warning in the Scripture about the danger of pride. If our hearts turn proud, we are heading for destruction. We need to pray the prayer David prayed when he asked the Lord to search his heart to see if there was any wicked way in it. We need to pray this so we can remain humble in our hearts. (See Psalms 139:23-24.) The Lord knows best what is in our hearts, therefore it must be our prayer for Him to search it and try us.

Pride is like bad breath; everyone can smell it, except for the one who suffers from it. Several years ago, something interesting took place. Whenever I stood close to my wife to talk to her privately, she would gently push me back a little. After this happened several times, I asked her to be very honest with me and tell me if I had bad breath. Knowing that pride and bad breath are the two things hard to detect by the one who suffers from it, I needed her honesty. She assured me that this was not the case, but that I was out of focus when I stood so close to her. Rather than bad breath being the issue, we discovered that she needed to get reading glasses. We all need help to keep our hearts free from pride.

6. Loosen Up

Also do not take to heart everything people say, lest you hear your servant cursing you (Ecclesiastes 7:21).

As we live our lives thankfully because the Lord is always ready to heal the wounds of our hearts, we need to learn what it means to watch our hearts. We grow in maturity as we follow the Lord. One sign of maturity and a healed heart is that we have learned not to take everything to heart that people say. This does not mean to live our lives arrogantly, not caring at all what anyone says. But Scripture admonishes us that in the multitude of counselors there is wisdom. Although hard at times, we can learn not to take to heart when people express their unpleasant opinions about us.

It is impossible for anyone to wholeheartedly follow the Lord without being criticized for it. For example, see Luke 6:26 and Second Timothy 3:12. We need to learn to turn all temptations to criticize others to the Lord in intercession and pray for the very ones we feel tempted to criticize. We must never forget that it is only by the grace of God that we stand.

It is my prayer that the Lord grants us the grace to receive healing for our emotional wounds. May He also help us to walk through the steps toward our healing speedily as we mature in Him. He desires for us not just to be people whose hearts have been healed by Him, but to be people who bring healing to countless wounded soldiers of His army and restore them to their purpose and destiny.

Walking in the Freedom of God

When we allow God to deal with any unforgiveness and bitterness in our lives and learn to receive healing for our wounded hearts, we will experience the joy of true freedom. The Lord delights in teaching us to quickly and freely forgive all who sin against us and let go of all offenses before they turn into bitterness. Doing this will result in the life of true freedom that God intends for us. We will not only be free ourselves, but we will also bring freedom to others. True freedom is being in the will of God, and it is His will for us to forgive all people their sin against us. Since *hurt people hurt people and healed people heal people,* we can become part of God's great army of love that brings healing to many. This world is full of hurting people who need us.

God delights in bringing glory to Himself by using people who have been rejected by others as weak, wounded, and hopeless. He doesn't need our strength, just our hearts surrendered to Him in childlike faith. He heals and restores us for this twofold purpose, because He loves us with an everlasting love, and He loves the rest of the world and wants to express this love through you and me.

It is my prayer that this book is part of what God is doing in your life to bring much fruit for His eternal Kingdom.

Reality Check

Do I love the Lord with an undivided heart? Which areas of my heart are not totally submitted to the Lord?

How often do I seek the pleasure of being in His presence?

Where and when do I worship the Lord?

Is there any pride in my heart? Which steps do I take to guard myself against it?

How can I learn not to take everything people say to heart?

Prayer

Lord, I thank You for Your amazing love for me. I can see clearly that You want me to watch my heart and keep it free from unforgiveness and bitterness because it is in my own best interest. I make the choice today and every day to live a life of forgiveness. I will always be quick to forgive those who wound me and release it all to You. Help me to walk it out every day of my life. Thank You. Amen.

ABOUT THE AUTHOR

If you would like to order copies of this book or
messages preached by Reinhard Hirtler visit
www.powertoforgive.com.

If you would like to contact Reinhard Hirtler
regarding a speaking engagement, please e-mail him at
reinhard@hirtler.net.

Additional copies of this book and other
book titles from DESTINY IMAGE are
available at your local bookstore.

Call toll-free: 1-800-722-6774.

Send a request for a catalog to:

Destiny Image® Publishers, Inc.

P.O. Box 310
Shippensburg, PA 17257-0310

"Speaking to the Purposes of God for this
Generation and for the Generations to Come."

**For a complete list of our titles,
visit us at www.destinyimage.com.**